Simply Better

Simply Better

Winning and Keeping
Customers by Delivering
What Matters Most

Patrick Barwise

Seán Meehan

Harvard Business School Press

Boston, Massachusetts

Library of Congress Cataloging-in-Publication Data
Barwise, T. P.
    Simply better : winning and keeping customers by delivering what matters most / Patrick Barwise, Seán Meehan.
      p. cm.
    Includes bibliographical references and index.
    ISBN 0-87584-398-0
    1. Customer satisfaction—Evaluation. 2. Marketing. I. Meehan, Seán.
  II. Title.
    HF5415.335.B37 2004
    658.8'12—dc22

                                            2003025723

To my family—PB

To Gill, Alice, and Emma:
This book would never have been
written without your support.
Thank you—SM

Contents

Preface

Sacred cows make the best hamburger.[1]

—Mark Twain (1835–1910),
U.S. humorist, novelist, short story
author, and wit

In today's competitive markets, conventional wisdom says that:

- The customer is king

- To compete successfully, you must offer something unique, but doing so is increasingly more difficult as physical products and services grow increasingly more similar

- The only solutions are to differentiate through branding and emotional values or to think outside the box and change the rules of your industry

There is some truth in each of those statements, but we think they have been overstated, which matters because it means too many businesses have focused on the wrong things. In our view:

- In principle, the customer is king, but it often does not feel that way if you are the customer! Ask almost anyone about his or her latest bad customer experience. Most can tell you about something recent like a beautifully designed new kitchen for which some wrong parts had been ordered, or the organization whose Web site or call center drove them to drink only last week, or a wireless network that gave them a new cell phone to use overseas that did not work, or the franchised car dealer that charged $1,000 for a service, returned the car with its steering wheel upside down, and then made the customer check it in again four days later so the garage could fix its own mistake. The list is endless and includes even the best, most admired companies.

- You need not offer something unique to attract business. Customers rarely buy a product or service because it offers something unique. Usually, they buy the brand that they expect to meet their basic needs from the product category—gasoline or strategy consulting or mortgages—a bit better or more conveniently than the competition. What customers want is simply better—not more differentiated—products and services.

- Branding and emotional values are great if you are already providing an excellent functional product or service. Outside-the-box strategy is terrific—when it works. But because even some of the best organizations are performing badly on the basics, we recommend that they start inside the box, ensuring that they reliably meet customers' reasonable expectations on the product or service itself. Once the basics are securely in place, the organization has a solid platform for great emotional branding and for more radical innovation.

This book is a back-to-basics manifesto for businesses—the majority, we think—that have failed to keep their eye on the ball, failed to listen to their customers, failed to deliver on the basics.

Despite such negativity, *Simply Better* is an optimistic book. We see the gap between the high-flown rhetoric and the disappointing reality of customer experience as a low-risk, high-return opportunity. If you read on, then you will see that we do not renounce differentiation, innovation, or branding—in fact, we discuss all three—but we emphasize that they must focus on what matters most to customers, usually the generic category benefits that all competing brands provide, more or less, and *not* unique brand differentiators. (Late in the book, we do add a tangential twist, that marketing communications such as advertising, promotion, and public relations must be distinctive to get attention.)

One problem—which we consider an opportunity—is that top management often fails to see the real issues, for two reasons. First, many top managers spend little time interacting directly with customers wherever they buy or use the product or service. Second, people usually tell their bosses what they believe their bosses want to hear, and the bosses do the same to their own bosses, and so on up the ladder. We believe that all managers should have regular direct customer contact. More generally, we discuss customer-focused innovation, employee motivation, and development of a customer-responsive culture throughout the organization.

The book carries two general themes. First, everything hinges on giving customers what matters most to them, even if that proposition seems less exciting than focusing on novelty, uniqueness, or the latest management or technology fad. Second, what separates winners from losers is usually not their strategies but their differing ability to execute those strategies. Most companies should first improve their execution and only then look for a better strategy.

Doubtless we have overstated, oversimplified, and overgeneralized in places. This book is for experienced managers, and so we wanted to keep it short. While readers may find some of it a little obvious, that is part of our point. As obvious as the *Simply Better* argument may sound, companies still struggle to focus consistently on customers, especially while simultaneously trying to reduce costs. We hope that you, the reader, will recognize enough opportunity in your own business to apply some of our arguments profitably, adapting them to your own particular needs.

Acknowledgments

This is a wide-ranging book, and we have many debts of gratitude. We wish to credit a few.

First, although we write for managers here, we base our work on the scholarly research and thinking of many business academics, acknowledged in the chapter endnotes. Here, we single out Peter Drucker, Andrew Ehrenberg, Gerard Tellis, and Peter Golder, whose research and writing most strongly influenced the ideas in *Simply Better*.

Secondly, several executives generously shared their experience to help us sharpen and validate our thinking. These include Pius Baschera, CEO of Hilti; Bill George, former CEO of Medtronic; Jacques Dubois, chairman of Swiss Re Life and Health America Inc.; and the senior management of Toyota Europe. Charlie Dawson, founder of consulting firm The Foundation, has been both a source of ideas and an excellent collaborator on our research into customer focus. We would like to thank John Howkins of Rainey Kelly Campbell Roalfe/Y&R and Anthony Bradbury of Land Rover for the Land Rover advertising example. Thanks too to Luc Imbert of Cereal Partners Worldwide; Chris Warmoth, formerly of Procter & Gamble; and Pat O'Driscoll of Shell for sharing their experiences and insights.

We would also like to thank the friends and colleagues who gave us valuable feedback on earlier drafts: Gordon Adler, Tim Ambler, Henri Bourgeois, Elizabetta Camilleri, Jack Carew, Jeremy Chandler, Sandy Geddes, Catherine Horwood, Esther Jackson, Parminder Kohli, Peter Lorange, Nancy Lowd, John Lynch, Cormac Meehan, Marco Mendes, Mope Ogunsulire, Katty Ooms-Sutter, Atul Pahwa, Michael Phelan, Janet Shaner, Craig Smith, Chris Styles, Nader Tavassoli, Simon Terrington, Dominique Turpin, and Morgan Witzel.

We have been supported throughout the project by Kirsten Sandberg and all her colleagues at Harvard Business School Press, who helped keep us focused, and by our colleagues at London Business School (LBS) and IMD.

Finally, our warmest thanks to the rest of the team—Margaret Walls and Sharon Berry at LBS and Barbara Schaefer at IMD—for their patience and professionalism in coping with endless drafts, revisions, charts, tables, endnotes, and permissions.

As the eighteenth-century critic Samuel Johnson said, "That which is written without effort is generally read without pleasure."[1] We hope that you will read *Simply Better* with both pleasure and profit, but if you do not, it will not be for lack of effort on our part—or help from those acknowledged here.

Simply Better

1

Differentiation That Matters

*Your company does not belong in markets
where it cannot be the best.*[1]

—Philip Kotler,
The S.C. Johnson & Son Distinguished
Professor of International Marketing at the Kellogg
School of Management, Northwestern University

Orange—Simply a Better Wireless Network

By the early 1990s, 6 percent of the U.K. population owned a cell phone. Analysts expected the market to grow at a staggering 75 percent per year until 1995 when penetration would reach 33 percent.[2] By any standards this market offered great prospects for two well-capitalized new players, One2One and Orange. Their opportunities were identical: exploit the overall market growth, attract first-time subscribers, and capture existing subscribers who were unhappy with the incumbents, Vodafone and Cellnet. One2One and Orange were awarded identical, simultaneous licenses and had access to identical technology. But their performance was far from identical.

In August 1999, Deutsche Telekom purchased One2One for £6.9 billion. Two months later, Mannesmann bought Orange for £20 billion. With a level playing field, Orange's superior strategy and execution had created almost three times as much shareholder value than One2One's had. What matters is not the absolute numbers—in hindsight, the financial markets in 1999 overvalued most telcos—but the ratio between them. Orange had simply gained more customers than One2One, and those customers were more valuable in terms of revenue, margin, and loyalty. The company achieved this by differentiating itself from its competitors in ways that mattered to customers. How did it differentiate itself?

Delivering and Improving Generic Category Benefits

The cell phone and the wireless network created a new category. They allowed users to communicate at will. Whether out for the evening and needing to contact friends, calling for a ride home, alerting someone of car problems, or just calling to chat, cell-phone users expect to get a signal, dial, and reach the intended number without being disconnected prematurely. Those criteria are the basics, and they relate to the expected functionality of the service. Other basics relate to how the service provider treats the subscriber, including offering a fair service rate and contract terms as well as helpful customer service.

As early as 1996, a Consumers' Association survey clearly set Orange apart from other players on the basics.[3] Although 14 percent of Orange subscribers reported that they could not always connect with the network, that figure was only half of the market average and almost a fourth of One2One's rate. All buyers expect decent treatment from a service provider; otherwise, they will likely defect—if they believe a competitor will treat them better. Eight percent of Orange subscribers said they would opt for a different network if they did not have to pay a penalty. That figure compared very favorably with the industry average of 27 percent and One2One at 32 percent. When J.D. Power and Associates rated user satisfaction in U.K. wireless networks in 1998, Orange scored 121—20 points ahead of One2One.[4]

By the time One2One and Orange launched their services in September 1993 and April 1994, respectively, Vodafone and Cellnet were well established, but subscribers had formed a negative image of the industry. Given the prevailing practices, that reaction was hardly surprising. According to the Consumers' Association report, service providers expected customers to sign "unfair" contracts.[5] Those contracts often stated that the provider could vary all or any of its charges while subscribers could not cancel their contracts without incurring a significant penalty. Providers charged calls by the full minute rounded up. Some contracts even disowned liability—if the network broke down, the customer still had to pay the usual service rate. Many customers were dissatisfied with the networks' low reliability. The most common complaints included successive failed attempts to reach the number dialed, weak reception and static interference, dropped calls, and crossed lines.

Enter Orange with its promise to provide a reliable, high-quality overall customer experience with good value for money—what the market wanted but was not getting. Orange offered per-second billing, a simpler rate plan, caller ID as standard, a money-back guarantee, and itemized billing free of charge. Per-second billing was not so much inspired as just fair and equitable. Competitive value to Orange came from being first to market with such a basic symbol of fairness. Such features as free itemized billing, free insurance, an extended warranty, a fourteen-day money-back guarantee, or a twenty-four-hour handset-replacement service were not the product of cutting-edge R&D; they were just plain common sense. At the time they were the features that delivered the brand promise—to provide the generic category benefits in a way others had failed to, and at a fair price. Orange learned from the incumbents and, seeing their failings, chose not to follow them. It took care of the basics the others had neglected. It gave customers what really mattered.

Serving the Whole Market, Not a Segment

The second key to Orange's success is that it targeted the whole market, not just a specific segment. By being the best at delivering the generic category benefits, Orange had an offer that was, by definition, suitable for the mass market. Its regional roll-out reflected that fact. The company launched in April 1994 with 50 percent national coverage. Within eighteen months that coverage rose to 75 percent, well ahead of One2One's 40 percent. By early 1996, Orange's network covered 90 percent of the population—almost on par with Vodafone and Cellnet, whose networks had long covered about 95 percent.

One2One's strategy had led it in a different direction. Seeking to differentiate itself from the incumbents, who still made most of their money from business customers, it positioned itself as a low-cost, friendly network suitable for people wanting to chat with friends. Since most personal calls are local, One2One put a priority on big cities. In London, it built twice the call-handling capacity of any competitor. By focusing its network on big cities, it was also able to launch a full seven months before Orange. One2One believed that, at this early stage in the market's evolution, it could use the time advantage and short-term capacity to build and retain a new customer base. It offered a unique deal: free off-peak local calls. Between September 1993 and March 1994, it gained sixty-four thousand subscribers—twice as many as Orange achieved in the six months after its April 1994 launch.

One2One's strongly focused targeting and differentiated positioning, however, backfired. Most of its customers were highly price-sensitive. Heavy off-peak free calls meant that One2One's annual revenue per customer (as of 31 December 1996) at £341 was lower than any competitor's. Meanwhile Orange led the industry with annual revenue per customer of £442. Further, heavy off-peak usage clogged One2One's network: Call quality and reliability suffered. One survey found that One2One either regularly or occasionally cut off about half of its customers for no apparent reason while they were stationary.[6] Two in every three users were regularly or occasionally unable to make a call because the network was busy.

Unfortunately for One2One, media interest in its network problems reminded customers of the importance of quality and reliability. The basics were center stage. The issue for Orange was to capitalize on this situation in the long term. It continued to push the boundaries on delivering category benefits better than anyone else. It kept on innovating. That commitment to innovation was the third key difference between Orange and One2One.

Continuing to Innovate

Strategists may well have been concerned to see Orange head straight into the market as the fourth player in a commodity business, with no silver bullet. Not one element of its offer was proprietary or complex enough to provide a sustainable advantage. Indeed in the two years after Orange entered the market, Cellnet, Vodafone, and One2One all copied several of its innovations. They also reduced prices aggressively. By early 1996, both Vodafone and Cellnet offered copies of Orange's bundled service rates. By then, Orange was about 5 percent more expensive than Vodafone and Cellnet and 20 percent to 30 percent more expensive than One2One. The short-term impact? For some time Orange didn't gain subscribers as rapidly as it could have. But Orange was not static, either. Year after year it came to the market with more commonsense features (see table 1-1). These post-launch innovations all represented market firsts. They ensured that Orange would continue to lead the category in providing the generic category benefits—that is, deliver the most reliable and high-quality overall customer experience with fair value for money. Continuously innovating on dimensions that really matter contributed to Orange's carving out its position in the U.K. market as "the most personable telecommunications company in the world."

Again, most of these features were not high tech; they were simple, utilitarian augmentations of the wireless offering, and they all left Orange open to competitive retaliation.

Orange's moves consistently reflected the brand values it touted from the start: refreshing, honest, straightforward, innovative, and friendly—values that the market had every right to expect of all players.[7] Those values had particular worth for Orange only because none of its competitors had adopted anything like its customer focus. And the company communicated its values through award-winning branding and advertising that

TABLE 1-1

Orange Firsts

Year	Innovation
1995	Two lines on one phone
1996	ISDN access
1997	Conference calling
1997	Prepay service
1998	Credits for calls disconnected by network
1999	Voice recognition
2000	Choose-your-own off-peak prepay rate
2001	Global flat rate for international calling

Source: www.orange.com

broke the mold for the category. Among other notable elements was the absence of cell phones in the company's advertising campaign. (We return to the important issue of Orange's communications strategy and what can be learned from its approach in chapter 5.) But the fundamental reason for Orange's continuing success well after its initial launch was that it was the first to deliver customer-focused differentiation—differentiation that matters. One2One, too, had a strategy based on differentiation, but it was the wrong kind. The difference between the two was worth £13 billion in shareholder value.

Customer-Focused Differentiation

Simply Better is about achieving differentiation that matters to customers.[8] This is certainly not a new idea. In the guise of the "marketing concept"—the idea that business success comes from meeting customers' needs better than the competition—Peter Drucker put customer focus on the management map just fifty years ago.[9] The broad thrust of his argument—that it makes sense to put customer value creation at the center of all activities—has long been well accepted at some level by executives. In 1988 the Marketing Science Institute prioritized research that explored the nature of market orientation and tested its relationship with business performance. The weight of subsequent scholarly evidence clearly supports the "customer first" argument. The research has repeatedly highlighted the importance of market sensing and an innovative, externally focused organizational culture.

Many examples have been reported to illustrate different aspects of market orientation. Ritz-Carlton, Pioneer Hi-Bred International, BP Nutrition, and Tesco have all been showcased for their ability to capture, understand, and leverage customer information. Attentiveness to customer service was held up as a hallmark of companies such as Nordstrom, Scandinavian Airlines System, and Lands' End. A customer-focused corporate culture, epitomized by the behavior of the CEO, is often a key factor in allowing companies to prioritize customers' interests in the face of pressure from competition: Intuit, Southwest Airlines, and Cisco are all well-known examples.

In spite of all the helpful frameworks, scholarly testimony, and inspiring examples, we characterize the marketing concept as being no better than well accepted at some level because customers themselves still report mediocre levels of satisfaction. Even the best companies continue to let their customers down far too often. All the change programs, the market research, and the statements from CEOs throughout the 1990s appear to have had limited lasting impact. We need to think customer focus through again and, this time, make it happen.

Persistent Customer Dissatisfaction

The American Customer Satisfaction Index (ACSI) is the world's most comprehensive assessment of customer sentiment. It makes depressing reading. Despite increased expenditures on customer satisfaction measurement and unprecedented discussion of the topic in the business press, aggregate satisfaction today is still lower than when the first study was conducted in 1994. We sometimes ask unsuspecting executives to review the summary trends (figure 1-1) and tell us what they see.

Comments generally focus first on the downward initial trend followed by a slow and less than full recovery. The discussion

FIGURE 1-1

**The American Customer Satisfaction Index
(Q3 1994 to Q3 2003) Indicates No Improvement**

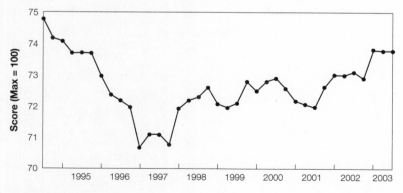

Source: www.theacsi.org

often moves to difficulties of measurement followed by that mother of all excuses—rising expectations. The usual story is this: "We live in a world where the customer experiences good service in, say, a bank and then expects his luggage to arrive with his flight. Rising expectations are something we cannot control, and, therefore, we are not to blame. It is someone else's fault."

We remain unconvinced and unimpressed. It is a waste of time and energy to agonize over why the index fell from 75 to 70 and only partially recovered. We need to focus on the bigger picture. Never, in the more than fifty times we have presented this simple chart, has the initial discussion pointed out what should have been blindingly obvious: These ACSI levels indicate a colossal opportunity for improvement.[10] Even high-scorers, such as Amazon.com with an index level of 88, run a risk of losing customers who are not fully satisfied. The cost of managing the fallout—refunds, returns, and bad word of mouth, not to mention the cost of new-customer acquisition—is enormous.[11] We believe that there is room for dramatic improvement in almost all industries. The good news is that this presents a low-risk, high-return opportunity for most businesses. *Low-risk,* however, doesn't mean low effort. Clearly, if fixing the problem was easy, many companies would have done so. We think there are two main reasons they haven't. First, meeting someone else's needs rather than one's own goes somewhat against human nature, especially if the other person either is reticent about expressing what she wants or criticizes our efforts to provide it. It requires effort, as well as empathy and imagination, to overcome this barrier. Second, there is often little incentive for people in organizations to make this effort. Creating a customer-focused business involves a combination of customer and competitor insight, employee morale, good systems, and the right culture—topics we discuss in the following chapters.

What Customers Want

We believe your *first* priority should be to improve performance on the things managers often dismiss as being mere "table stakes," "hygiene factors," or "order qualifiers" (as opposed to "order winners") and that we will refer to as the "basics." Most customers, irrespective of how you may have organized them into segments with slightly different needs, expect the basics. Alas, it seems they are disappointed remarkably often. The rewards that would arise from businesses simply meeting and exceeding straightforward, reasonable expectations are substantial.

By achieving differentiation that matters Orange created significant shareholder value. It mainly succeeded by providing the basics better than the competition. Those criteria included network coverage (getting a connection), network reliability (not getting cut off), and transparency or trustworthiness (being charged only for what you use). Those are basic, and they are usually valued more than some unique brand benefit offered by the competition, even something as costly to provide as One2One's free local off-peak calls.

Every company serious about customer focus should aim to be the best at the things that matter most to customers. That is the secret of Toyota's rise to the top of the automotive industry—"excluding gimmicks and pursuing the essentials."[12] It is the secret of Cemex's remarkable success in cement, which is usually seen as a textbook commodity business: Above all else customers simply want the right kind of cement at the right time and place. Construction workers who want to be sure that they have an efficient, reliable power drill call for a Hilti. And in the grocery industry, which is so open to fast imitation, Tesco emerged from the pack to become number one in Britain by offering a superior shopping trip to everyone. Ryanair, responding to the mass market's desire for really cheap air travel, became Europe's fastest-growing, most profitable, and most highly valued airline by focusing exclusively on that goal—offering the lowest fares; that's all, no extras of any kind.

These successes can of course be attributed to many factors. We want to ensure that one surprising factor is not overlooked. These companies all chose to be the best at some basic things that most of their competitors could also have done. Those things, taken together, mattered a lot to most potential customers. They were *generic category benefits*—those benefits most customers expect most of the time and for which, in practice, performance can vary.

That definition is important because it helps us understand that, although generic category benefits are often written off as mere table stakes, they are not: Performance on the basics can vary enough between competitors to dominate all other sources of differentiation. The companies we have mentioned all focused primarily on providing the basics better than the competition. Over time, through continuous improvement, they redefined what was achievable and expected. Customers saw them as different—but different as in simply better, not as in unique or different for the sake of being different.

The Primacy of Categories over Brands

The simply better approach applies almost universally. Its focus on generic category benefits reflects how buyers actually choose between competing and often very similar offers. Research on buyer behavior suggests that, from a customer perspective, product categories matter more than individual brands. We return to this key issue later. For now, we note that the evidence is that, although understanding customers' priorities and choice processes is a critical element of business success, in too many companies it is still not the focus of executive energy.

To reengage with customers, executives must think explicitly about categories, for it is within categories that competition is manifest. A category is a set of competing choices that, as seen by the buyer, share some key characteristics and provide broadly similar benefits.

You have found the real category benefits sought by customers when you are clear about the category's boundaries. These boundaries define the upper limit of customers' *consideration set*—the set of competing brands they actively consider when making a category purchase. For example, in the United Kingdom in the mid-1990s, consumers wanting mobile communication service might have considered the offers of up to four wireless networks.

In other cases, the category definition is less clear cut. Consider cereal bars. They are simply bars in which the principal ingredient is cereal and that, through their form, offer convenient consumption. Although different brands primarily identify the bars as providing energy-, weight-loss–, health-, or snack-related benefits, they are often lumped together by analysts and merchandisers in a single category. But that isn't so helpful. According to Luc Imbert, marketing manager at Cereal Partners Worldwide (or CPW, a joint venture between General Mills and Nestlé), recognizing children's basic need for great taste and parents' basic need for nutritional reassurance led to kids' breakfast-cereal bars containing recognizable bits you normally find in boxes of breakfast cereals. CPW introduced Chocapic bars, Golden Graham bars, and Nesquik bars with great success. In this case the category is kids' on-the-go breakfast. The direct competitive set is clear, although there is also competition from other products—for example, some other packaged snacks and fresh fruit, such as bananas.

Category definitions, then, are not always clear cut, nor are they set in stone. And all customers don't have the same needs nor the same willingness or ability to pay. But providing the main current category benefits better than the competition is a sound starting point for most businesses.

Consider Hilti, which creates and sells drilling, demolition, and fastening solutions for construction and building maintenance. Hilti does not serve a single segment: Its market is all professionals in construction and in building maintenance. To quip that "customers don't buy a drill, they buy a hole" does not help. The basic category benefit sought by all construction professionals is to enhance effectiveness and productivity. Hilti competes on that basis, which does not mean that there are not segments or that segmentation cannot be helpful. As with many business-to-business (B2B) markets, Hilti's customers vary enormously. Hilti segments the market based on dimensions, such as the size of the business the professional works for. There are many differences in needs and buying behavior between a self-employed artisan and one working for a big construction company. However, it is the basic category needs, constant between segments, that dominate Hilti's strategic thinking, product development, and delivery systems.

Segmentation and differentiation are often a distraction. Innovators must take care that the brand-specific benefits they provide are not trivial, peripheral, or relevant only to a small minority of customers. The technical and design achievements of the makers of the thoroughly innovative, differentiated smokeless cigarette or the similarly unique see-through refrigerator door failed to make mass-market successes of their offerings because most customers just did not care.

Category Benefits—
More Than Just Table Stakes

Consider the following hypothetical (and oversimplified) scenario. You plan to enter a market. The issue is how to develop and position your offer. Figure 1-2 shows customers' perceptions of the eight established brands against the two main attributes for the category (the number of attributes does not affect our argument). The size of each circle represents the size of that brand. Where should you position your offer?

If your primary concern is unique brand-specific differentiation, you will look for a gap in the market, most likely the bottom right on the chart. Here customers are likely to perceive your brand as highly differentiated. Your unique positioning is low on Attribute 1 and high on Attribute 2. The disadvantage is that, assuming the positioning map is based on sound research, the gap your competitors seem to have missed is so obvious. Either your competitors are all being stupid, or positioning here and achieving a profitable margin is not feasible. For instance, One2One's distinctive initial positioning largely excluded it from

FIGURE 1-2

Where Should We Position a New Brand?

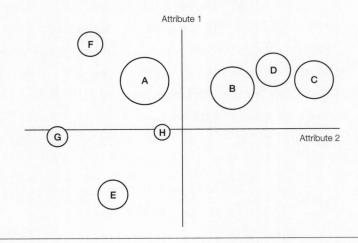

the business market and high-value consumers. More than ten years later, One2One (now T-Mobile) still has lower revenue per user than its competitors and struggles to make money.

Alternatively, there may be no demand for your particular unique attribute combination—or perhaps customers find it hard to believe, like a low-calorie food product that tastes great and is easy to prepare, or a high-performance car that is also safe and economical. Positioning in the gap may be both feasible and profitable, but there are often good reasons why the gap exists. In figure 1-2 this suspicion is reinforced by the fact that E and G, the two most differentiated brands in the chart, are also two of the smallest.

If instead you ask, "Where is the ideal point for most customers?" (this is a researchable question, at least for the current market), the answer is most likely somewhere in the space that includes A and B, the top two brands. Or the market may be segmented, with one segment dominated by A and the other by B, D, and C. Either way, by positioning in this region you will likely face the competition head-on and seek to trump it. Such a plan of attack goes right against most conventional wisdom in strategy and marketing, but it might be the right strategy, based on the right kind of differentiation. We encourage you at least to consider this because, in the words attributed to bank robber Willie Sutton when asked why he robbed banks, "That's where the money is"—as Orange showed.[13]

Of course, successfully capturing the high ground of the market is not easy (nor, we imagine, is successfully robbing banks). It requires insight into customers' perceptions, motivations, and behavior; the ability to identify opportunities based on current and potential category benefits; and outstanding execution—innovation, customer focus, and communications. We cover all those issues in the rest of the book.

Generic Category Benefits Versus Unique Selling Propositions

Conventional wisdom often says that one of the foundations of success is providing a unique brand-specific customer benefit, popularly referred to as a unique selling proposition (USP). Examples include Crest with its anticavity protection and Volvo with its leading-edge safety features. Many companies do provide unique brand-specific customer benefits, but few of those benefits have led to a large, sustainable competitive advantage. Even with the benefit of legal protection, many good ideas are easily copied. For instance, air miles, bonus points, and other gifts that were introduced to "incentivize" loyalty were quickly copied by competitors and became an expected (and for the companies, very expensive) component of any airline or car rental offer. Most outlets that offer film-developing services to traditionalists now also offer one-hour film processing. Thanks to competition, high-speed development is today seen as a basic service even though it was a unique customer benefit when first introduced.

In a competitive market, category benefits are by definition not unique. Every business aspiring to compete in a given segment must provide them to an acceptable degree. All viable hotel chains provide safe shelter, warmth, a clean bed, and bathroom facilities. Automobile brands provide reliable transportation. Major food retailers provide a reasonable variety of food that is fit for everyday consumption. The same is true in B2B markets. Architects and specifiers, although they recognize and appreciate speed and high-tech gizmos, have a duty to ensure that the elevator they specify and install in a new building is safe and will work reliably around the clock. They also need to know that the model ordered will arrive precisely on-site, on schedule, and in good condition; that the invoice will be right the first time; and that after-sale services, such as planned maintenance and breakdown repairs, will be efficient and reliable.

Dominating a perpetual niche can be a rewarding strategy—ask Velux, the world's leading manufacturer of roof windows and skylights; Tetra, world leader in tropical fish food; Hauni, which makes most of the world's cigarette-manufacturing equipment; or Gerriets, which holds a virtual monopoly on color-neutral lighting cloths for theater stages.[14] Those companies know that their continuing success depends on their ability to deliver the category benefits, and this book may have little to teach them.

Such examples are rare and limited in scale, however. The general pattern is that a business can achieve long-term growth only by competing in a large and/or growing market and by reliably delivering the generic category benefits better than a range of strong, competent, well-resourced competitors. *Simply Better* is for businesses in that challenging situation.

Reliably Delivering Category Benefits

Habitual usage accounts for the predictability of revenue streams and the tremendous value of many big, established brands. To support such habitual usage, companies must ensure that their brand is perceived to deliver the category benefits better and more reliably than acceptable substitutes. Customers value that certainty. We conducted a study in which consumers described some of their recent purchases in their own words.[15] Again and again, they talked about both large and small brands reliably delivering the category benefits they wanted: One consumer said he chose Gillette Sensors over other disposable razors "because they have worked in the past, and they're a reasonable price, . . . tried and tested, and not horrendously expensive."

Another interviewee explained how a clothing store delivers its category benefits:

> *I had been asked to buy a quality cashmere sweater as a gift from another member of the family to yet another member of the family. And I thought, "I'll try the Burlington Arcade.". . . And N.Peal is the first shop as you go in, and I thought, "Oh yes, I'd forgotten N.Peal, and that's all they do—quality cashmere and standard of service and product. And you are able to exchange things later."*

One reason why most new packaged-goods brands fail is that it takes such a large investment of time and money to change a consumer's habitual behavior. Many of the top brands from eighty years ago are still market leaders: Examples include Coca-Cola, Campbell's, and Wrigley's.[16] This is why the trend, even in packaged goods, is for companies like Procter & Gamble and Unilever to focus their resources on a smaller number of big, established brands. Similar issues can apply in B2B markets ("no one ever got fired for buying IBM") with the additional factor that there are often many switching costs that make customers reluctant to change suppliers.

Routinized, unconsidered buying does not diminish the importance of the category to customers. In daily household life, there is nothing unimportant about cleaning clothes, maintaining healthy teeth, or putting dinner on the table. When one of those activities fails to go smoothly—the shirt collars were not clean; the ready meal was inedible—annoyance, cost, and wasted time usually follow. Familiar brands reduce risks in a reliable, affordable, convenient way. Their suppliers act swiftly and decisively if anything goes wrong. That response is expected. In late 2000, computer giant Dell recalled some twenty-seven thousand notebook-computer batteries after one had overheated and caught fire. In February 2002, Schering-Plough recalled batches of its best-selling allergy drug Claritin-D because the tablets did not dissolve fast enough in water. In other well-publicized cases, Firestone recalled 6.5 million tires in 2000, Ford recalled nine hundred thousand vehicles in 1997, and Coca-Cola withdrew a hundred thousand cases of soda in Belgium. Reputation, or brand equity, does not appear on the balance sheet, but when necessary, you must be prepared to spend heavily to preserve it because of its long-term impact on revenue and margins.

Innovating to Meet and Exceed
Evolving Expectations

All-time business heroes include the likes of Sam Walton, Ed Land, and Jack Welch. They are people who successfully redefined categories, created great new products, and rethought their business models. We admire these innovators because they addressed real customer needs, both realized and previously unrealized. Few will enjoy this kind of success, but a good way to increase your chances is to focus first on innovating like Orange to deliver the category benefits more reliably than the competition. That approach then provides a solid platform for an established brand to introduce new lines, new forms, and even extensions into new categories, as long as they meet and reinforce positive consumer expectations. We interviewed one person about her decision to use Standard Life for her pension. She explained:

> *Right, the reason that I went [with Standard Life] was because I was desperate to get out of the Equitable [another pension provider that was in some serious financial difficulty at the time] as fast as possible. I can't stand so-called independent financial advisors, and I'd had very good experiences with Standard Life. . . . When we had a mortgage with them, they were the best in the field over a long, long period—like two decades. And, finally, they have a AAA rating from Moody's or [Standard & Poor's], probably both.*

An especially fruitful area is those needs that the customer knows but that are still unmet, either because they have not been identified by the companies in the market or because the companies have failed to address them satisfactorily. It's a mistake to focus too much on how a brand or business is performing against the competition at delivering the benefits already identified by the industry. Doing so results in missing the opportunity to gain ground on the competition by broadening the basics—that is, by providing an important previously unidentified or insufficiently met category need better than the competition. As Orange showed, broadening the basics (e.g., by introducing per second billing) would often provide more return than other more speculative, albeit perhaps more exciting, work in new or emerging markets. We return to this theme later.

Genuine customer-focused innovation is rarer than one might expect. It would be more prevalent if companies focused their innovation on identifying and providing category benefits better than the competition. Executives should beware the buzz around latent needs. Ever since Emerson's infamous better mousetrap, and doubtless long before, we have had no shortage of business ideas that cropped up before their time.[17] They fail mainly because the alleged latent needs turn out to be so trivial, or to apply to so few customers, that the resulting market opportunity is minimal or nonexistent. There is no potential new category. And the fear of losing the opportunity to be the first mover should not spook executives. The sustainable advantage has been shown to accrue typically to the second or third entrant with the vision, courage, and capital required to create or redefine a category.[18] JVC and Procter & Gamble did not lead the market in VCRs or disposable diapers, but they did create mass-market categories by focusing on innovation to meet and exceed real needs and expectations.

The dot-com boom produced many examples of the opposite. The now defunct HeavenlyDoor.com, touting itself as the "portal of e-smart solutions for the aging" (code, we suppose, for pre-funeral planning), allegedly burned through $22 million before accepting that seniors and their families were not interested in the service. Shipping dog food, barbecue supplies, and so on, all failed the brutal realities of the customer marketplace. In the words of business historian Morgan Witzel, "I grow very tired of people not only reinventing the wheel, but making it square because this is a new and exciting feature. The 'new' business-to-consumer e-commerce model was usually just Montgomery Ward's mail order catalog reinvented and badly executed."[19]

We have nothing unique to say about how to assess new venture proposals: Everyone knows that radical innovation is extremely risky and that the key issues are whether the new venture meets a significant latent or emerging need and whether management is good at execution. The judge is the market. Later we describe the approach of Tesco.com in developing its online offer—which it always saw as just another way to provide the category benefits to its customers. It was not that Tesco uniquely identified the opportunity. Remember Webvan, the online grocery service? In just three years, Tesco.com and its home-delivery service has grown to cover 95 percent of the United Kingdom, receives 70,000 orders each week, and has annual sales of more than £300 million, about 10 percent of all online retail commerce in the United Kingdom. It is the largest online grocer in the world, and it makes money.

How Customers Really See Your Brand

Simply Better rests on a specific view of customer behavior: that customers rarely buy a brand because it offers a unique feature or benefit. Rather, they usually buy the brand that they perceive as offering the *best overall combination of category benefits*—or, if they really see no material differences, as simply the cheapest, the first they see, or the first they remember. This is a hard lesson. Executives care passionately about the unique features of their offer, hanging on to facts like "our fax machine has the smallest footprint in its class." Customers rarely share this passion. The painful truth is that the differences between competing fax machines are far more important to those who make them than to all but the most geeky customers. The same is true in almost every category.

Suppliers and buyers live in different worlds. For the supplier, the only thing that matters on a particular purchase occasion is whether the customer buys the supplier's brand and at what price. This is a winner-take-all game—no prize for second. All the revenue goes to the brand the customer buys, none to any other brand. The difference between winning and not winning is everything.

To the customer, the world looks different. Usually, the purchase is triggered by a simple need, such as the need for a small bag of cement for a house addition or a business hotel for two nights in Chicago. The customer meets the need by making a category purchase. What the customer actually buys is a brand, but what he or she wants or needs is the category. If gasoline disappeared, the United States would grind to a halt. If Exxon gasoline disappeared, who would lose out? Exxon employees, dealers, and shareholders. An extreme case? Perhaps. But the contrast between the importance of the category to customers and the relative unimportance of even the strongest brand is not so very different in other categories, such as cars, PCs, fast-food restaurants, and credit cards. To the supplier, the only thing that matters is the brand (how many sales? at what price?). To the customer, the only thing that matters is the category (does it meet my need? is it available? at what price?).

This view runs counter to much of the conventional wisdom about competitive positioning and differentiation, but it is certainly not a counsel of despair. It forces us to be realistic about what is feasible yet still leaves plenty of scope for beating the competition and creating shareholder value. *Simply Better* requires top management to rethink how to compete. Innovation is still crucial, but it's directed more at improving the delivery of the generic category benefits and less at trying to develop unique brand benefits. And execution is usually more important than strategy.

Structure of the Book

We devote the next chapter to looking at how customers see your brand and make purchase decisions—the source of all shareholder value. In chapter 3 we show how executives can translate this understanding of the buying process into an informed view of what customers really value—what the generic category benefits are, and maybe could be, in a given category. It is these benefits that should drive resource allocation and innovation and, in turn, drive the market. Chapter 4 then discusses management challenges to such innovation, focusing on motivating employees and developing the right business systems.

In addition to management challenges, being simply better also raises a challenge for marketing communications. It is harder to communicate that your business or brand provides the same benefits as the competition, but better, than to communicate a unique benefit or USP. It is not a coincidence that an advertising man, Rosser Reeves, first proposed the USP concept, nor that many of its advocates even today, such as Al Ries and Jack Trout, started in advertising. Advertising people naturally look for something unique to say about the brand to make it easier to stand out from the crowd.

We address the communication challenge in chapter 5. We argue that, although the main focus of the product or service offering should be on generic category benefits, communications about the brand should be creative and distinctive, to cut through the clutter of other communications bombarding the customer. Communications about the brand include advertising via both traditional and new media, sales promotion, direct mail, and public relations. This is an area where out-of-the-box thinking really is valuable.

Jim Collins and Jerry Porras, in their best-selling book *Built to Last*, show that few great companies started with a revolutionary new product. Instead, long-term success came from a clear and enduring set of values that formed the basis of innovation and execution year after year, in good times and in bad.[20] Being simply better is a never-ending story, a grind with vision and purpose. In chapter 6, we cover some of these so-called soft issues. We explore the role of core values and beliefs in enabling an organization full of talented and ambitious people to stick doggedly to identifying category benefits and delivering on the basics simply better than the competition. The resulting customer-focused mind-set underpins all the processes described in chapter 3 through chapter 5.

Finally, chapter 7 briefly reviews the argument of the book and suggests six rules for putting it into practice.

Doesn't It All Depend?

We are not arguing for a one-size-fits-all strategy. We agree with those who say, "Well, it depends." However, our observation is that the simply better idea resonates with executives in businesses serving relatively mature stable markets, such as Toyota, Cemex, and Shell, as well as with those in high-growth markets, such as that of Orange and Medtronic. It may be particularly important for small players, if they are to succeed, to have at least as good an understanding of the important category benefits as the market leader does. This will help those small players gain maximum leverage from their more limited resources and market presence.

Of course the details of how to compete depend on the context. But we really are arguing that the starting point for every business should be to identify and deliver the generic category benefits better than the competition. We hope that, by the time you finish the book, you will agree.

IDEA CHECK

Is your approach to differentiation customer-focused?

1. What are the main benefits you deliver for your most important customers?

These are generic category benefits. If you cannot name a small number with complete certainty, you are not customer-focused.

2. Do you deliver these for all your customers?

You should deliver the generic category benefits to all—perhaps to varying degrees, depending mainly on customer value. Some customers are much more valuable than others—some may even be costing you money—but your starting point should acknowledge that they are all looking for much the same category benefits.

3. Do your competitors also offer these benefits?

If they do not, then these are not generic category benefits—try Question 1 again.

4. How regularly are you monitoring your performance on these benefits?

You should do so obsessively; providing these benefits well and as dependably as the sunrise is why customers keep coming back.

5. Are you proud of being simply better?

You should be. Get over wanting to be unique; it may be exciting, but it probably does not drive business success.

2

How Customers
Really See Your Brand

*Marketing is not a specialized activity. It is the whole
business seen from the point of view of its final result,
that is, from the customer's point of view.*[1]

—Peter Drucker,
American management thought-leader,
writer, teacher, and consultant

Alliance & Leicester Building Society—
The Power of Customer Insight

For most of us, most of the time, mortgages are boring. The exception is on the few occasions when we are buying a new home.
Motivated by fear that something could go wrong, we then combat our boredom, wade through the small print of offers we can
just bear to look at, decode the broker's patter, and hold on tight.
Research supports the notion that we crave reassurance that we
will be safe. One rule we use is that bigger is better. We will give

the benefit of the doubt to financial institutions of an acceptable size. For example, in the United Kingdom, 86 percent of people said that if they were looking for a mortgage or a savings account, they would consider only a major bank or a top-ten building society, the U.K. equivalent of a U.S. savings and loan association.[2]

Immediately before their 1985 merger, the Alliance and the Leicester were, respectively, the ninth and tenth largest U.K. building societies. It was expected that the new Alliance & Leicester (A&L), now the number-six player, would become a more powerful force. The opposite transpired. Within two years A&L had actually lost market share, and its margins were reduced. A&L was in crisis. The issue was, what to do about it? The main initial solution came from a possibly surprising source—advertising, despite the fact that savings accounts and mortgages are not the most fertile territory for great advertising.

The Advertising Challenge

Most advertising by savings and loan associations (S&Ls) and building societies is seen by people who are not in the market at that moment and are, therefore, completely uninterested in the advertised products. Even if an ad does happen to catch a prospective customer at the right time, there is little if anything it can say to differentiate the brand functionally from the competition. You know the conventional wisdom in advertising: Focus on something—anything—that uniquely differentiates your brand or products from competitors'. But there is nothing you can say about the number-six building society's products that will interest home buyers, even when they are in the market. The category is boring, the products are very similar, and the regulations quite rightly forbid unsupportable product claims.

A&L decided it would be impossible to develop an effective campaign based on functional product claims, and the company's cost base would not allow it to differentiate on price. The obvious alternative would be to use advertising to add emotional values to the brand. Many banks and other financial services companies have tried to do that, with an extremely low success rate. Consumers have seen dozens of campaigns showing grateful customers and delighted-to-help bank staff, with a warm, upbeat (but not wild) music track and a voice-over babbling on about how wonderful and friendly the bank is. Everyone smiles like members of a North Korean dance troupe. If you watch one of these ads with the sound muted, often you have no idea even who it is intended for since there is no visual branding until the last frame.[3]

If very well executed, these campaigns can help at the margin, at least by encouraging the staff to be a bit nicer to customers. But an emotional branding campaign in financial services requires a big budget, long-term investment, and really outstanding creative work—plus parallel investment in staff training and probably in branch refurbishment and technology. Even then the advertising investment is extremely risky, given the low success rate of this type of campaign. The emotional branding route, therefore, looked as unattractive to A&L as the functional product claims route.

Consumer research provided the key customer insight that enabled A&L to escape from this impasse. The research highlighted the critical role of brand familiarity in consumers' purchasing of financial services:

- Most consumers would consider financial products only from a limited number of institutions they believed to be acceptable.

- The key criterion for acceptability was perceived security.

- Perceived security was a function of perceived size.

- Perceived size was a function of familiarity. If a bank or building society was highly familiar (high unprompted awareness), it was assumed to be large, secure, and, therefore, acceptable (figure 2-1).[4]

The Advertising Campaign

Based on this customer insight, A&L and its ad agency devised a series of award-winning TV commercials using British comedians Stephen Fry and Hugh Laurie to increase awareness of the A&L brand name. Fry played a pompous, arrogant buffoon who always ended up in trouble after trying to use either

FIGURE 2-1

Customers Are More Likely to Consider Familiar Brands

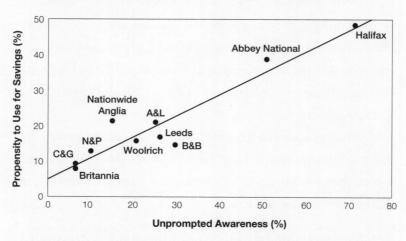

Source: Chris Baker, ed., *Advertising Works 7* (Henley-on-Thames, Oxfordshire: NTC Publications, 1993), 363.

the latest and most complicated or the cheapest financial products. In contrast, Laurie was the sensible A&L customer who got a reliable result with no fuss. The tagline was "You get a smarter investor at the Alliance & Leicester." Although the campaign did mention A&L's size and products, it aimed to increase the number of customers who included A&L in their consideration sets simply by increasing the company's awareness level.

In the five years that followed the campaign's launch, A&L's unprompted awareness (the percentage of people mentioning it when asked to list building societies) rose from 18 percent to 24 percent. Prompted awareness (where customers are shown a list of brands and asked which ones they have heard of) increased from 52 percent to 86 percent. The number of consumers who considered A&L an acceptable provider of mortgages more than doubled to about seven million. Its share of total mortgagees—normally a very stable metric—increased from 6.9 percent to 8.0 percent in just three years. A&L had become significantly more likely to be in the consideration set of mortgage seekers when that rare purchase occasion arose.

The Fry and Laurie campaign was well liked, something that tends to make advertising more effective, but the main reason why it worked is that it made consumers more familiar with A&L's brand name, which in turn made them more likely to include it in their consideration set.[5] It was crucial that the campaign was based on a specific insight about how consumers buy financial products.

The A&L story is partly about great creative advertising but mostly about how a company used its understanding of how customers buy and use the category to get itself out of a tight spot.

Understanding the Customer

All shareholder value comes from customers buying your brand, usually in competition with other brands that they might have bought instead. Understanding customers' priorities and choice processes, the subject of this chapter, is, therefore, fundamental to long-term business success.

We start with the controversial assertion that customers do not expect your brand to be unique. This view underpins our argument that companies should mainly focus on improving their delivery of generic category benefits, which matter to customers, rather than on looking for unique brand-specific differentiators, which customers usually regard as trivial.

We then discuss the idea that customers do not care much about your, or your competitor's, brand. Their main concern is to simplify their lives, partly by limiting the time and effort they spend on most purchases—which helps account for the fact that they do not see most brands as strongly differentiated.

The key question, which we then address, is this: If customers do not see competing brands as strongly differentiated, why do some brands sell so much more than others? Part of the answer is that even small differences in brand preference can, if held by enough customers, lead to large differences in market share. Other factors include price, distribution, and familiarity. With A&L, we have already illustrated how familiarity can affect whether customers include a brand in their consideration sets, but we will also discuss an important further effect—that, other things being equal, customers usually *prefer* familiar brands.

There are some cases where a particular product or brand is perceived as unique, especially in creative industries like fashion and music. We briefly review some of these exceptions to the general pattern, as well as the more widespread situation where a brand achieves a degree of uniqueness by offering a different combination of category benefits from the competition. Every brand and its situation are unique—hence the need for customer research and other forms of market sensing—but we urge you not to generalize from these exceptions.

In the final section of this chapter, we briefly describe how companies compete to win customer purchases via the product or service itself, distribution, price and sales promotions, and marketing communications. This discussion leads into the following chapters about how simply better organizations identify and exploit market opportunities based on generic category benefits.

The Uniqueness Myth

Contrary to much conventional wisdom, buyers rarely look for uniqueness. Price, availability, and familiarity often matter a lot. But because customers know that all the brands in their consideration set are pretty similar, they use simplified choice routines.

Marketers' obsession with unique brand differentiators goes largely unnoticed by customers and, even when noticed, rarely convinces them. In most categories, consumers do not have strongly differentiated images of the various brands, except for simple descriptive attributes (e.g., Mountain Dew is known for its caffeine intensity) that do not greatly discriminate between people who do and do not buy the brand. People are likely to remark on more evaluative attributes that do matter (e.g., Mountain Dew tastes nice) about the brands they buy, and, partly but not only for that reason, they are more likely to say those things about the biggest brands.

The size of a brand is largely a reflection of how many category users believe it delivers the main category benefits. "In a survey of U.K. toothpaste, an estimated 55 percent of customers of the brand leader, Colgate Dental Cream, thought that it 'Promotes Strong Healthy Teeth,' and a very similar 57 percent of customers of the eighth biggest brand, Ultrabrite, thought that about their brand, despite Ultrabrite's radically different positioning based on whiteness."[6] The main explanation for the relative size of each brand was that substantially more consumers attributed this ("promotes healthy teeth") and other category benefits to Colgate rather than to Ultrabrite.[7]

In other words, customers either do not notice or, if they do notice, do not care about most of the differentiators that brand marketers often fuss about. The implication is that strategists should not try to make their brand different for the sake of being different. They should focus on providing the benefits—regardless of the extent to which the competitors provide those benefits, too—that matter to the customer. Doing so is often harder work than adding a unique, trivial differentiator (e.g., making the toothpaste pink) but is usually the only way to create shareholder value through differentiation, as opposed to low price.[8] Tackling this challenge is where real innovation, which creates differentiation that matters, comes in. Let us take a closer look at how such innovation affected the highly competitive U.S. toothpaste market.

Toothpaste Wars: Crest Versus Colgate

By the early 1990s, Crest, with its anticavity proposition, had achieved a U.S. market share of 30 percent. Colgate had a 19 percent share, and Aquafresh 10 percent. In 1993 Unilever launched Mentadent, which for the first time combined baking soda and peroxide, two ingredients long associated with dental hygiene, using a novel two-pump package. In less than two years, Mentadent was a $250 million brand with a 12 percent market share.

Colgate Total launched in the United States in 1997. Within four years Colgate had gained 18 percent to become the new market leader with 37 percent. As its name suggests, Colgate Total claimed to offer everything. Colgate's traditional strength was its flavor. In addition to great taste, Colgate Total offered breath-freshening and whitening power and dental health, thanks to triclosan, an antibacterial agent that when combined with fluoride, helps prevent tooth decay, plaque, and gingivitis. Colgate Total's success was not based on a single unique differentiator; it was based on providing what the market saw as the best overall package of category benefits.

Even advocates of USP-based strategy admit—and bemoan—that brands are becoming less differentiated. One of the best-known is Jack Trout, who dedicated his apocalyptic book *Differentiate or Die,* published in 2000, to Rosser Reeves, the marketer who originally proposed the USP concept. Together with marketing consultant Kevin J. Clancy, Trout asked U.S. consumers whether they perceived forty-six pairs of leading brands (e.g., Visa/MasterCard, Nike/Adidas, Mobil/Shell) as having become more differentiated or more similar. In forty out of the forty-six categories, consumers responded that the brands were becoming less distinct.[9]

Clancy and Trout blame marketers for this reduction in perceived differentiation, saying, with some justification, that too many have diverted money away from long-term brand building to short-term price promotions that do nothing for brand equity, that is, customers' positive feelings and beliefs about the brand.[10] In our view, however, the main explanation is simply that consumers are increasingly resilient to marketers' attempts to differentiate their brands through advertising and, in most cases, simply do not care.

The Law of Double Jeopardy

Buyer-behavior patterns also reflect the lack of perceived differentiation. There is a myth that, through clever targeting, positioning, and advertising, a small brand can create a profitable niche within a category by dominating the category purchases of a small minority of customers. In practice, that phenomenon virtually never happens. Instead, the pattern is that small brands suffer from the Law of Double Jeopardy: In a given time period, they not only have far fewer buyers than big brands do, but they usually also have a slightly lower average purchase rate.[11]

Table 2-1 illustrates the double-jeopardy pattern for toothpastes in 1996, just before the launch of Colgate Total. For instance, Crest's 29 percent market share came from 28 percent of households buying it on average 2.1 times in that year.

The main difference between the big and small brands in table 2-1 is that many more people bought the big brands over the year. In addition, consumers bought those brands on more purchase occasions. Most small toothpaste brands aim for a niche positioning, but none of them achieved that in terms of having an especially high average purchase frequency. The closest was Sensodyne, for people with sensitive teeth. Even it had a slightly lower purchase frequency (2.0) than the average of the top four brands (2.1). Further analysis shows that households

TABLE 2-1

Small Brands Do Not Dominate a Market Niche

Top twelve U.S. toothpaste brands in 1996

Brand	Share %	% Households Buying	Average Purchases	
Crest	29	28	2.1	
Colgate	22	20	2.1	average 2.1
Aquafresh	12	14	1.9	
Mentadent	8	9	2.2	
Arm & Hammer	6	8	2.0	
Ultrabrite	3	4	1.9	average 1.8
Listerine	3	6	1.5	
Pepsodent	3	3	1.8	
Close-Up	1.9	3	1.7	
Aim	1.8	2	1.9	average 1.7
Sensodyne	1.5	3	2.0	
Oral-B	0.6	1.4	1.3	

Source: Information Resources, Inc.

that bought Sensodyne also bought other brands more than twice as often: It did not dominate the purchases even of those households.

The pattern in table 2-1 is typical and has been replicated many times.[12] Most so-called niche brands are just small, not different in their purchase patterns. The exceptions are where a brand meets a very specific set of needs, which perhaps many customers have occasionally, that other brands do not meet. For instance, Velux's main product is a particular type of double-glazed window that, when closed, fits flush into a sloping roof but also hinges in the middle for easy opening. Conceptually, it is better to think of Velux as a big brand in a niche category (i.e., roof windows and skylights) than as a niche brand in the general window category because its products have limited substitutability with most other windows.

As we noted earlier, in some other categories, especially foods and beverages, these distinctions are less clear cut. For instance, is lemon-lime soda a separate category? We would argue no because it is closely substitutable with other sodas, but this is clearly a matter of degree and not, in our view, crucial. Defining the category too narrowly becomes a problem only if it encourages people to ignore significant market developments at the periphery.

How Much Buyers Really Care About Your Brand

Often, our biggest mistake as managers is believing that, in general, customers care a lot about our brand. They do not. They care about the benefits our brand and competitors' brands deliver. All other things equal (including price and availability), customers buy the brand they think will deliver the category benefits the best. The process works like this: Consumers realize they need to make a category purchase—gasoline, yogurt, a DVD player, or whatever. Their prior knowledge greatly influences which brand they then choose. Usually, that information includes knowledge both of the category and of the brands that are most likely to meet their needs. In fact, many purchases rely so much on what the customer remembers that they require no real thought: You are next to the yogurt section in the store, you need yogurt, you see your favorite brand in its usual place, and you put it in the shopping cart—done.

Simplifying Buyers' Lives

The fact that customers rarely bother to compare all the competing brands or to use all the available information, even about those they do consider, means that their behavior falls short of economic rationality, which would ordinarily assume that they would use all the information on every brand before making their choice. But time is limited, shopping around is usually a chore, and favorite brands work pretty well, so routinized buying behavior seems to us extremely rational. In the words of mathematical philosopher Alfred North Whitehead: "It is a profoundly erroneous truism . . . that we should cultivate the habit of thinking of what we are doing. The precise opposite is the case. Civilization advances by extending the number of important operations which we can perform without thinking about them."[13]

What is true of civilization as a whole is also true of us as individuals: We advance partly by increasing the number of things we can do without having to think hard about them, from walking and talking to driving—and shopping. With most of those activities, we sometimes do stop and think a little, but our lives are greatly enriched by the fact that, most of the time, it is only a little.

Major Purchases

Even major purchases depend on impressions, unconscious memories, and intuition. Buying a home is a huge decision. Yet from the time people see a house to the time they decide they would like to buy it is often just a few seconds. A long process of information gathering, reflection, anxiety, discussion, and so on follows that decision, but the buyer's reactions during those first few seconds likely strongly influence the final choice. That is why realtors encourage sellers to spruce up the front flower beds and the entrance hall.

The same can be true of organizations buying brain scanners, hiring management consultants, and making other corporate brand choices, including recruitment: First impressions matter. The main difference in B2B is that the decision makers spend the organization's money, not their own. The amount involved is typically much larger than most consumer purchases. The decision process is more formalized, and its results are more likely to be explicitly monitored. It may require complex technical as well as financial evaluation and will likely involve several or many different individuals. In fact, a salesperson selling a brain scanner—or a consultant selling a new project—may in practice be mainly providing ammunition to help his or her allies in the buying organization make a persuasive case for a positive decision, with the salesperson's company as the supplier. Single individuals make few major organizational buying decisions; it is usual to talk in terms of a "decision-making unit," consisting of people from several functions, each with his or her own agenda. The B2B marketer must work to ensure that the brand is there when the competitive pitch takes place. Despite these complexities, the underlying process is the same as in business-to-consumer (B2C) purchases and includes generic category needs, a brand consideration set, and brand choice.

Considering Only One Brand

Such is the urge for simplification that in practice, customers—especially consumers—often consider only one brand. One study found that, even for cars, 22 percent of French buyers had a consideration set of only one brand, usually the brand they already owned.[14] This is remarkable. A car is a very high-ticket purchase that, unlike mortgages, also involves most buyers emotionally. It is an infrequent purchase in a category with fairly frequent model changes, so the competing alternatives usually differ from those that were available the last time the consumer bought a car. But, still, more than one in five car buyers considered just one brand. A few of those buyers may have been fanatically committed to the brand and, therefore, did not consider any others. Our hunch is that most were simply too uninterested or too busy, or believed that the competing brands were all pretty similar.

For most consumer categories, the proportion of purchases to a consideration set of just one brand is likely to be a lot higher than it is for cars. For routine repeat purchases of many packaged goods, it is likely close to 100 percent. That fact helps account for the great stability of year-on-year market shares in those categories.[15]

Big Differences in Market Share

If customers rarely perceive brands as strongly differentiated, why do market shares vary so much? It is not at all unusual for the market leader to be ten or twenty times bigger than the number-five brand.

Sometimes, the explanation is price. If two or more acceptable brands are perceived as equally available and equally good but their prices differ (e.g., because one is on special), the customer will usually buy the cheapest. One person we interviewed explained his decision to buy a refrigerator at a particular electrical store: "Before I decided Curry's, I did actually shop around, on the Web and through Wal-Mart, [and I] spoke to people. . . . Curry's had the best deal . . . [including] six months interest-free credit. . . . That was a pulling point really." Another interviewee described choosing a bookstore, once again with price as the deciding factor: "We'd actually been into the Borders a few doors down from WHSmith's, and had a look and seen that there were certain books we wanted, and thought we'd try Smith's first before buying them and found a few other books in Smith's that we wanted. [Author: Why Smith's rather than Borders? The price is the same, isn't it?] No, because Smith's [is] doing a lot of three [books] for £10."

Price, however, is also perceived as an indicator of quality, so a customer will sometimes pay more on the assumption that you get what you pay for. Here's what one interviewee had to say about price:

> *Author:* How do you distinguish between different *petits pois?*
> *Interviewee:* Price.
> *Author:* OK, but was Tesco's the cheapest?
> *Interviewee:* Yes
> *Author:* Suppose the store had an economy one?
> *Interviewee:* No, I probably wouldn't have bought the economy one.

Wal-Mart got to be the world's biggest retailer with a business model that relentlessly drives down its unit costs and passes most of the benefits on to consumers in lower prices. But for every Wal-Mart, there is a Coca-Cola, a McKinsey, a Microsoft, or a Cemex, market leaders whose prices are as high as or higher than most of their competitors'.

In the glory days of Big Blue, IBM had a 60 percent share of the world market for mainframe computers. That market share was certainly not driven by price: It was said that if an IBM proposal came with a lower price than a competitor's, at least one of them had misunderstood the specifications or messed up the quote. Nokia, Intel, Cisco, PricewaterhouseCoopers, Boeing, Disney theme parks, Mercedes trucks and buses, and HBO did not become leaders by undercutting the competition. Price is rarely the explanation for the disparity in market shares.

Another factor is distribution. If the customer sees no meaningful differences between several acceptable brands and believes any price differences to be too small to justify the effort of shopping around, he or she will simply buy the first brand seen. Consider these examples:

The car was out of petrol, and that's my nearest petrol station.

[Carlsberg Export] was the only premium export lager in [the pub] and, therefore, the only premium lager and, therefore, the only lager I would buy. [Author: And were you influenced by the Carlsberg brand?] No, there was no other lager in there, so if it was a no-name lager, I still would have drunk it.

Sometimes, even in today's competitive market, it takes time and effort for the customer to find the first acceptable brand:

The skirt I needed for a specific occasion—to make an outfit. I had a jacket, hat, and shoes. I, therefore, needed very specifically a black knee-length skirt. I had been all over in my shopping bit of London and had been quite unable to find one, and this was the last shop I was going to. [Author: How many did you try?] Oh, about half a dozen—I was more than ready to give up.

Obviously, in services such as retailing, fast food, auto repair, and mass-market hotels, brands can vary enormously in their number of outlets. Similarly, sales of physical products and even of entertainment products, such as movies and consumer magazines, depend on how widely those products are distributed. A movie's first-week box-office revenue correlates strongly with the number of screens showing it. Distribution is especially important for impulse or convenience products like snacks or razor blades, which is why companies such as Mars, Frito-Lay, Kodak, and Gillette take trade sales, logistics, and merchandising so seriously. But for established brands within a national market, distribution rarely explains the large long-term differences in market shares.

In the short term, there is a chicken-and-egg relationship between distribution and final sales: You need distribution to get consumer sales, and you need consumer sales to persuade distributors to stock your brand. But in the long term, it is mainly final customers' brand preferences that determine the distribution, not the other way round. If McDonald's and Holiday Inn franchisees and Kodak and Frito-Lay retailers did not make money *selling* those brands, they would switch to selling others. And the reason they make money is customers' final brand choice.

This relationship is especially clear for established brands of packaged goods, such as breakfast cereals or toothpaste. Typically, the top brand and the number-five brand are both available in at least 80 percent to 90 percent of supermarkets, but the first outsells the second by a factor of three or four, and sometimes much more.[16]

Small Differences in Brand Preference Can Lead to Large Differences in Market Share

Paradoxically, the lack of strong perceived differentiation means that small differences in brand preference can lead to large differences in market share. If a consumer thinks Colgate Total is 10 percent better than Crest, she will not buy 10 percent more Colgate than Crest; she will *always* buy Colgate unless it is out of stock, Crest is on special, or she wants Crest for a change. Colgate's and Crest's relative market shares largely depend on how many consumers think each brand is a bit better than the other. Neither group's brand preference is strong: A Crest buyer would be annoyed to run out of toothpaste but quite happy to buy Colgate instead or on special because he knows that it will provide much the same category benefits to much the same extent.

When two brands are about equally available and equally priced, the customer in principle buys the one for which the expected benefits best match the benefits sought from the category. For example, historically, Crest has tended to emphasize fighting plaque and cavities while Colgate has emphasized flavor. Other brands might emphasize breath-freshening (e.g., Close-Up) or tooth-whitening (e.g., Ultrabrite) abilities. To the extent that consumers care about these product attributes and believe the manufacturers' claims, they tend to buy the brand that they think will best deliver the particular mix of benefits they seek. But in practice, they are usually pretty uninterested in and skeptical about such claims. So, if they find a brand that does the overall job well enough, they will likely become a repeat buyer.

One manifestation of consumers' lack of interest in the differences between brands, and of the fact that small preference differences can lead to large disparities in market share, is that market shares can vary enormously between local markets. Bart J. Bronnenberg, a marketing professor at UCLA, found large and persistent market share differences for packaged-goods brands in local markets in the United States.[17] For instance, two brands might have had market shares of 40 percent and 10 percent, respectively, in Los Angeles and 10 percent and 40 percent in New York. Further, these variations were greater for relatively undifferentiated categories, such as mayonnaise, than for more differentiated categories, such as breakfast cereals. Bronnenberg concluded that each brand owner is unwilling to attack its rival's strong markets for fear of provoking a retaliation in its own strong markets, especially when the brands are almost undifferentiated.

Being Considered

Getting your brand into customers' consideration set, by no means a trivial step, can be one of the main factors that determine brand share. The first precondition for breaking into a customer's brand consideration set is usually awareness—the focus of the A&L advertising campaign.[18] The second precondition is the customer's perception that the brand will reliably deliver the generic category benefits.

Even a minor purchase of, say, a small gift could in principle involve at least four steps after the recognition of a perceived need (i.e., "I ought to bring something with me when I visit the Harrises tonight"):

1. Generating a category consideration set (e.g., flowers, wine, or chocolates)

2. Choosing a category (e.g., chocolates)

3. Generating a brand consideration set (e.g., Neuhaus or Godiva)

4. Choosing a brand (e.g., Godiva)

With most purchases, however, the steps between perceived need and purchase are simpler than those. Although there are exceptions, at least 90 percent to 95 percent of the time customers consider just one category; the perceived need leads straight to a decision to buy the specific category. Perceived need implies category choice: If your car's fuel tank is low, you need gas, not charcoal or electricity. Usually, therefore, the consumer skips Steps 1 and 2 and doesn't generate a category consideration set or choose a category.

Most consumer research has focused on brand choice (Step 4), often starting with a list of brands and exploring how consumers whittle that initial list down to a single preferred brand. Increasingly, however, researchers recognize that generating a brand consideration set (Step 3) can be as important for the final purchase as brand choice within that set. A&L's advertising worked almost entirely because it increased the number of prospects who included the brand in their consideration set. It made virtually no attempt to differentiate the brand from the others in that set, for example, in terms of product features, price, service, or availability.

What do we know about how consumers generate a brand consideration set? Research shows that they use a combination of three methods:[19]

1. Scanning the available brands displayed at the point of purchase

2. Drawing on their prior brand knowledge (brand equity)

3. Actively searching

Unless they positively enjoy the search process—as some consumers do for such categories as cars, apparel, and electronic equipment—customers will save time and effort by relying on some combination of the first two methods if they can. For instance, the simplest way to buy wine or beer in a supermarket is to buy your favorite brand, especially if it is stocked in the same shelf as before. If it is not there, you will probably look at what is there and choose something you know or believe to be similar based on your prior knowledge. Further, once customers see or remember a brand that they believe will meet their needs satisfactorily, they simply pick that brand unless they think another will be significantly better or just as good but significantly cheaper.

Salience

If several acceptable brands are equally available at about the same price and the customer sees no meaningful differences in their perceived benefits, he or she will usually buy the most salient brand, that is, the one that is most familiar and comes most readily to mind. Managers working in a particular market for fifty hours a week often underestimate the power of salience.

Leading researcher Andrew Ehrenberg argues that salience is the main reason why a market leader is often ten times as big as, say, the sixth biggest brand: "[Salience] is the common factor in how many people are aware of the brand (by any measure), have it in their consideration set, regard it as value-for-money, buy it or use it, and so on. This then correlates with distribution, shelf space, market shares, and sales."[20]

What matters is brand salience or awareness relative to the competition. You may be aware of six courier services and regard them all as equally good, but if Federal Express and its telephone number are top-of-mind, and assuming it consistently provides a satisfactory service, you will likely use it again and again, based largely on its salience; it stands out from the crowd without necessarily having any uniqueness. And every time you use it, you will be reinforcing its salience in your mind.

In markets with high perceived risk for the buyer, such as cars, mortgages, and capital equipment, customers usually consider only brands with which they are already highly familiar. Less familiar brands are excluded from the consideration set even if the customer is already somewhat aware of the brand and even if a full evaluation would show it to be competitive in terms of expected benefits and value for money, which was precisely the issue A&L successfully addressed by increasing consumer awareness of its brand.

Brand Familiarity and Customer Preference

In addition to the consideration set and salience issues, there is a direct link between brand awareness and brand *preference* (i.e., the chance of being chosen against other brands in the consideration set), especially for low-involvement purchases. Social psychologist Robert Zajonc discovered this so-called mere exposure effect in a classic experiment in the 1960s using randomly assigned nonsense words, such as *Biwojni* and *Saricik*. Amazingly, even with these meaningless stimuli, subjects preferred those to which they had been briefly exposed several times over those that they had not seen before or had seen only once or twice.[21] Similar experiments support the overall conclusion: At least up to a point, familiarity increases liking. Did you know that most Parisians hated the Eiffel Tower when it was built? Imagine the reaction if you now proposed to demolish it. Apparently, Mexican babies hate chili con carne, but adult Mexicans are miserable without it. Familiarity matters.

Beyond a certain but, unfortunately, hard to predict point, however, further exposure can make something too familiar to people, and they start to dislike it. Overfamiliarity, in effect, breeds dislike (although rarely the proverbial contempt). Advertisers call this phenomenon "wear-out." It might partly explain why big brands do not always keep growing. Perhaps Coca-Cola is *too* familiar for some people, so more exposure does not make them more likely to buy it. For the Coke brand team, the challenge is to remain relevant to loyalists. In practice, though, very few brands have the problem of overexposure, so almost all publicity is good publicity.

Do Not Generalize from Exceptions

There are exceptions to these general patterns of customer choice. For instance, in many creative and entertainment industry categories, such as movies, music, books, and furnishings, every product is unique, and finding exactly the right one can be important to the customer. Some places, such as a particular hotel or restaurant, are special, as one interviewee pointed out:

Pen-y-Gwrd Hotel charges less than most B&Bs for the bed. The bedroom, it has nineteenth-century baths with twenty-first-century plumbing attached to them. Huge ones. It has excellent dinners, which cost more than the bed for the night, I think. The dinner is absolutely wonderful. And because it's . . . you know it's unique. It's where the Everest climbers trained. It has a lot of character.

Some brands are linked to a specific institution, where a substitute just will not do. Consider this comment:

The Gunners' Shop [which sells Arsenal Football Club memorabilia] is quite different. . . . There's only one Gunners' Shop.

Some products' appeal comes from the consumer's response to a specific design, flavor, or other factor, as these comments illustrate:

I saw [the shoes] and fell in love with them and had to have them. I tried them on and spent quite a long time deliberating whether I wanted to spend £60 on a pair of shoes.

[Author: Why did you choose the New Look top? You "found yourself" in the store again?] I did. [I'm an] impulse buyer. I liked it. I had an outfit that it could be worn with. It was a bit different, different from the run-of-the-mill tops that are everywhere. It was gingham, and without being too frilly.

In some cases, the design may just happen to be right for a particular occasion:

> *I chose that [birthday card with a picture of an elephant] because the little girl has a toy elephant that she's quite fond of.*

In creative markets simply working, no matter how customer-focused you may be, won't guarantee a simply better performance. Here the top talent, including performers, sports figures, and best-selling authors, creates and captures much of the value. Steven Spielberg, Tom Cruise, and Tiger Woods are major brands in their own right. Hiring Spielberg to direct a movie will give it a USP—but at a high price.

In some cases, as this comment shows, a combination of generic benefits and a USP drives brand choice:

> *I chose [the Maypole Garage] because they're local, because a friend used them and said they were helpful, and one of the key reasons is that they don't patronize women.*

A garage that does not patronize women is, sadly, still unusual. The auto market is gradually coming to terms with the importance of women as car owners as well as influencers, but for now, it is a USP in the respondent's local market.

Again, a customer may happen to value a specific brand benefit that is unimportant to most others:

> *I'd bought [that cat food] before, having read all the labels in the shop [and chose] the one that seemed to have the highest fish content. . . . My cats really like it, so I stuck to it.*

In most of these cases, however, the benefit (here the percentage of fish content in a cat food) would be easy for the competition to match if it appealed to more customers.

If customers do not buy the cheapest, the most salient, or the first available brand among several brands perceived as equally good at providing the generic category benefits, they usually buy the one they perceive as providing the best overall *combination* of category benefits, such as the range of offer, store layout, location, and comfort. Consider these comments:

> *The staffing policy [is impressive]—everyone is helpful, there is always someone there to help you pack, carry things to your car. There's a very high quality of goods, fresh and interesting, reasonable amount of organic stuff, which I like to buy. Big wine selection. I enjoy shopping there, as opposed to finding it a terrible chore. And they have a very good return policy, no questions asked.*

> *With Boots, they're accessible, nearly everywhere you go, and just outside the work place as well. The products are good quality. And Boots has its own brand . . . as well—good quality and good pricing. And plus I have the option of using my Boots card, so I can collect loyalty points.*

Is it fair to attribute these choices to preference for a unique amalgam of category benefits? In providing them these companies were not obsessing over the uniqueness of their offer. They—like Tesco, Toyota, and Hilti, all of whom we will look at in more detail later—were dedicated to providing a simply better total solution. They still focused on the generic category benefits.

How Buyers Choose
and Companies Compete

The generic model in figure 2-2 depicts what the customer wants, knows, and expects, and how he or she chooses. It reflects our category-first perspective and the impact of customers' simplification process. It also shows how companies compete to win sales through the marketing mix, those activities (in the shaded ovals) aimed at encouraging customers to choose their brand.

The key element is the *product* or *service* itself. It determines the extent to which the benefits the customer experiences from brand usage meet—or even exceed—the benefits sought and expected when the brand was bought. Was the new car as reliable as claimed? Was it a pleasure to drive? Did the after-sales service meet expectations?

Marketing communications usually focus on building brand equity although they can also be used to reinforce or trigger a perceived need (e.g., "call stimulation" in telecoms, which encourages customers to use the phone more) or to communicate price or availability ("New York return for only $99," "Delivery guaranteed in 24 hours"). *Distribution,* including managing the lead times on delivering orders, focuses on availability. Frito-Lay ensures not only that its products are widely available but also that they are usually fresher than the competitors' products. Coca-Cola built its global dominance on a relentless focus on distribution, providing product "within an arm's length of desire"—which has, in turn, strongly reinforced its brand awareness and equity around the world.[22] *Price* includes price promotions, payment terms, and issues such as which TV channels to bundle together at each price point.

FIGURE 2-2

How Buyers Choose and Companies Compete

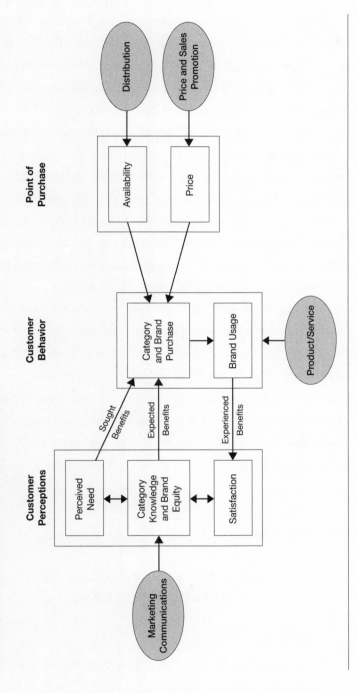

Customers' brand knowledge, or brand equity, comes from their total brand experience. In addition to brand usage, that knowledge also includes their experience of brand communications, coverage, word of mouth, and casual interactions with the brand, such as seeing a new car in the street.

Business-to-business markets are different but less so than you might expect. In fact our proposition may be even more compelling in B2B. The principal difference, as already noted, is that the buyer spends organizational, rather than personal, money. Usually, too, the buyer and user are different people, so the connection between user satisfaction (with a corporate IT system, say) and the buyer's brand knowledge is indirect. This situation often also happens in consumer markets—and not only for pet food.

In all markets, the challenge is to provide a product or service, competitively priced and distributed and well supported by marketing communications, in such a way that the customer experience reliably meets or exceeds expectations, leading to repeat purchases by the same customers and positive word of mouth to others. In the following chapters we discuss how to make that happen, starting with how companies identify the generic category benefits that matter to customers.

IDEA CHECK

How good is your understanding of customer choice?

1. What's your USP?

You do not have one? Good. It is not what customers are thinking of when they buy.

2. How top-of-mind is your brand when buyers think of the category?

If you are not in the top few, you will lose out dispropor-tionately.

3. Does your board have an explicit, shared model of how and why customers buy your category, generate a consideration set, and choose a brand?

It should. Such a model puts you all on the same page and enables you to focus your energy on what really matters.

3

Identifying Generic
Category Benefits

Fortune favors the prepared mind.[1]

—Louis Pasteur (1822–1895),
French biologist and bacteriologist

Hilti—Using Direct Customer Contact to
Reveal New Market Opportunities

Hilti is a world leader in developing, manufacturing, and marketing high-quality power tools and fastening systems for the construction and building maintenance markets.[2] The company's 2002 revenues, from more than a hundred countries, were about $2 billion.[3] Hilti serves the professional market; its customers include large and midsize construction companies and smaller independent contractors. It reaches them directly through seventy-five hundred technical sales representatives (TSs) who make seventy thousand calls daily. The TS is a key part of

Hilti's value proposition, offering advice and support to professionals, mostly on-site, and providing a channel for direct, timely feedback about new products and services.

Opening Up the Retail Channel

Alain Baumann, general manager of Hilti France, believed that Hilti should also reach individual tradespeople via a non-Hilti retailer. Although this segment was large and knew and liked Hilti, it was too fragmented for TSs to reach economically. A retail network could fix that problem. To make such a radical move, Baumann would need the support of Hilti's executive board, which would not be easy because such a proposal might threaten a core element of the brand and create channel conflict. It might dilute the strategic focus. In the end, the desire to deliver what matters most to its customers guided Hilti.

To professionals, Hilti is synonymous with its direct salesforce of TSs. Baumann proposed having TSs operate a shop-in-shop in a new chain of stores operating under the brand name La Plateforme du Batiment, owned by French multinational Saint-Gobain. La Plateforme was to be aimed exclusively at the professional construction market. To reduce the possibility of significant channel conflict, price consistency was carefully managed, and the trade-customer relationship was transparent. Baumann could negotiate an attractive deal because the retailer's research showed the Hilti brand to be very powerful in the professional segment—a brand from which La Plateforme would benefit.

The board supported the initiative. A key factor was the speed and force with which Egbert Appel, the board member responsible for finance and administration, backed the proposal. The day he had spent accompanying Pierre Legrand, a TS based in Paris, on routine sales calls to construction sites strongly influenced Appel's opinion.

The morning started at 5:30 in a parking lot. Before setting off in the distinctive Hilti van, Legrand asked Appel to wait a few minutes; he was expecting a customer to show up. The customer, a self-employed plumber, needed some new equipment. As Appel and Legrand made their way through the slow Paris traffic to their first site visit of the day, Appel inquired further about the customer. Legrand explained that the self-employed small-tradesperson sector was a big market, but TSs would never achieve their sales targets pitching to small tradespeople. However, once the TS got to know them, he could refer them to Hilti centers and customer service for follow-up. Because many of these small customers were constantly on the move, the arrangement also suited them.

The executive board agreed to proceed cautiously. Baumann could roll out the concept gradually in France, learning and adapting as he went along. Over eighteen months, the concept was introduced in all of La Plateforme's stores. There were no big surprises. It was notable that four out of every five customers using the shop-in-shop were new to Hilti.

It was not until 1998, three years after Appel's meeting with the plumber, that the importance of the French experiment became clear when Home Depot tried to interest Hilti in supplying its huge chain of U.S. stores. Now, armed with its experience of the practicalities of the shop-in-shop model, Hilti entered negotiations with Home Depot.

Although Home Depot was not looking for blanket coverage of its thousand stores, the scale of the exercise made it risky for Hilti. After much analysis, research, and debate, the executive board decided to approach Home Depot opportunity as it had done in France—one step at a time, with a cautious rollout, testing hypotheses as it proceeded. The French experiment has proved an invaluable experience in addressing the Home Depot opportunity.

All four members of Hilti's executive board regularly go into the market to listen to their customers. On average, each spends fifty days a year in the market. Depending on the size of the market and prevailing concerns, any number of the executive members go on a particular visit, which generally lasts two days. The first day is spent riding with a TS on sales calls. As well as talking with at least ten customers about service issues, repair speed, technical support, and product performance, the board member hears firsthand from frontline employees.

Getting into the Underground Mining Market

In October 1998, executive board member Ewald Hoelker, visited South Africa, home to some of the deepest gold mines in the world. Hilti had been asked to develop a new concept, a revolutionary electric mining power drill. The Hilti drill would be lighter, faster, and quieter and would vibrate less than the current standard. It would improve both efficiency and operator comfort. On paper, Hilti saw a big opportunity, but exploiting it would take the company into the unfamiliar world of underground mining, an environment with extreme safety risks. With Hilti uncertain how to proceed, Hoelker decided to go see the operational environment for himself. It was an unforgettable customer visit.

Hoelker squeezed himself shoulder to shoulder with more than a hundred miners into a two-story industrial elevator, dropped nine thousand feet into the deepest mining system in the world at a rate of fifty feet per second in the pitch dark, and then hiked four thousand feet, through temperatures reaching 100 degrees Fahrenheit, to the drilling area. There he observed the extreme working conditions miners had to endure. Typically, three men worked on bended knee in tight spaces four feet high and a few feet wide. Two hauled a heavy drill into place and held it steady while the third operated it. The noise was ear-splitting. According to Hoelker, "The decision to go into mining was huge. Although it all looked good on paper, . . . what really did it for me was seeing with my own eyes the enormity of the opportunity, the conditions those guys have to put up with, and seeing first-hand the current situation."[4]

From that moment in 1998, Hoelker became one of the main champions of the initiative. As of 2004, the project is in an advanced stage of commercialization. Within a few years, mining will likely have a significant place in the Hilti portfolio.

At first glance this may appear to be a radical step for Hilti. We do not see it this way. Hilti moved confidently here, as they did with the distribution innovations in France and the United States, because the company knew that it was being true to what real customers and users had to say, what they really cared about, and what would drive their future purchases. It is through this customer-focused lens that Hilti sees its business.

In this chapter, we examine the more effective practices for identifying generic category benefits. We start with direct customer contact: immersion in the market. We next discuss the complementary need to understand your competitors, which turns out to be a significant influence on business performance. We then look at category issues beyond yourself and your competitors: Exploring customer experience, and especially dissatisfaction, with the whole category can reveal new market opportunities. Finally, we discuss what happens when a USP, unusually, creates and defines a whole new category.

Immersion: Asking the Customer Directly

In the words of spywriter John Le Carré "A desk is a dangerous place from which to watch the world."[5] Most major companies today have some form of customer contact program for senior executives. Often these are initiated by the CEOs who then take very visible leadership roles. This was certainly the case with Herb Kelleher of Southwest Airlines and Jack Welch's so-called customer awareness trips at General Electric designed to ensure that all plant employees have a better grasp of how the customer uses the product (helicopter engines). Niall Fitzgerald, co-chairman of Unilever, has been a loud proponent of staying in touch with real customers (we'll discuss this in more detail later). Here it is helpful to note that the initiative spreads throughout the vast organization. New recruits at Hindustan Lever spend weeks living in villages to experience their customers' lives firsthand. An organization designs customer-contact programs to energize itself with ideas and a sense of relevance and urgency. Such programs are usually the best way for managers to engage with what customers really care about. Many customer-contact programs, however, are ineffective.

Ineffective Customer-Contact Programs

Despite prominent role models and accessible best practices, one study revealed large variance in companies' understanding of what should go on during customer visits.[6] CEOs were asked to describe how they allocated their time. The CEOs of the 100 best-performing companies in the sample (in terms of market share, sales and market share growth, profitability, and return on assets) spent a lot of their time—18 percent—in direct face-to-face contact with customers. But the equivalent amount of time for CEOs of the 100 worst-performing companies was, to our surprise, 15 percent—not much less. What is going on?

Follow-up interviews revealed a qualitative difference between the nature and value of the contact of the high and low performers. The CEOs of the low performers spent much of their time with customers socializing at cultural or sporting events. While entertaining may help solidify some relationships, it does not present a good context for useful customer feedback. CEOs of high performers, on the other hand, were less interested in such socializing; they wanted to get down to business and, especially, to know how their company was performing relative to its promises and the customer's expectations. They also persistently asked their customers how they could do better.

Considering All Customer Feedback, However Trivial It Might Appear

We all know that we cannot do everything. We certainly cannot do everything we would like to straight away. Strategy, after all, means choice. It is not unusual for CEOs who put themselves in front of real customers and clearly signal their genuine interest in customer issues to hear of very minor issues that simply annoyed a particular customer. Such minor issues often relate to something that happened recently and is top-of-mind—today's pet peeve. It may be an irritation the customer constantly hears about from his people and feels like venting about. Or it could be something major that is a consequence of some hard-to-see process failure.

In one recent case, a technology company lost a top client whose staff had not installed a tiny software modification issued by the supplier, causing the client's whole system to go down for twenty-four hours. The supplier's client support team had informed the client's people but had not followed up to check that they had installed the update nor told their own technical sales colleagues about it. Nonurgent modifications are now released quarterly so that everyone on both the client and the supplier side knows when to expect them and to check that they have been installed. The problem here may well have arisen before in some smaller accounts, but the technology company took no systematic action until that problem arose in a key account, at great cost to both businesses.

In all cases there is no evidence that the complaint is representative of all customers' experiences. Executives always work to a conscious or unconscious agenda that prioritizes the few things that they want to deal with. Organizationally, the planning process will have the same impact—priorities are set on the basis of someone's view of what is urgent and important. So, what is the role of the "sample of one"?

One-off samples of one are not scientific evidence. However, when executives collect such anecdotes regularly and build a clearer understanding of the customer's experience, individual customer problems or complaints can become a powerful change mechanism. Given strategic clarity and a thorough understanding of what the basics are and how you can deliver them simply better than others, you should consider all negative feedback customers deem worthy of offering when they are face-to-face. In most cases, you should ask someone to own the problem, discover the cause, fix it, and report back to the top.

Recently, the chief accountant of a consumer-goods company sat down with his counterpart at a major supermarket chain and heard that the customer's accounting department considered the statements and invoices he had regularly issued utterly unhelpful. In the big scheme of things he might have been tempted to think that this was a minor issue. Not for that customer. It was clear that his opposite number expected more. In the comfort of his own office, the consumer-goods accountant would never have realized that the paperwork he had designed could have caused so much frustration. Once skeptical about the value of customer contact for him, as a back-office person, he was now converted.

Executives have told us that when you put yourself on the firing line and you have made it clear that your interest is genuine, you will hear a lot, and you will often hear it with passion. It could well be passion that accounts for the particular effectiveness of this feedback channel and that makes it, for some, too scary to handle. Learning, after all, comes from negative, or at least challenging, and, therefore, uncomfortable feedback. And that kind of feedback is painful. In the words of Columbia University's Don Lehmann, "The term 'learning organization' implies being exposed to things you're not comfortable with. If everyone is comfortable, they're not learning anything."[7]

Fast Reaction to Market Information

Although one is often counseled not to be reactive, we advocate fast reactivity to market information. Bill George, former chairman and chief executive of medical technology leader Medtronic, was aware of some quality problems with a recently acquired manufacturer of angioplasty products, but he did not fully appreciate the frustration levels of the surgeons who had to use those products until he directly observed a procedure one day.[8] When it was time for the surgeon to insert the device, it literally came apart in his hands. He turned to George and threw the catheter, covered with the patient's blood, straight at him. In the aftermath, George asked the salesman, who was also there, whether this had ever happened before. Indeed it had—a few times. The representative noted that reports of such failures were filed regularly. One had been filed on this specific issue a month earlier, and Medtronic had still not responded. Reviewing the incident, George found that such a report had to work its way through eight people or departments before the quality manager even knew about it. With all the power of his office, George set out to fix this problem, drastically simplifying the report-back procedures.

CEOs and other top managers want to know what is going on. When they have products thrown at them, are yelled at, or are spoken to with a tone that says, "I trusted you guys to get this right. You let me down; I'm hurt," they do not want a repeat performance. So, armed with evidence from just one incident, the CEO returns to base, demands an explanation, and makes it clear that such an incident will not happen again. Generally, it does not. The problem goes away not only for the customer in question but probably for all the others affected by it. Simply, the willingness of the CEO to be out in the market with customers, at the unfiltered front line, is an important source of quality and performance improvement.

Why Immersion Works

This kind of direct customer feedback is called *immersion*.[9] It fuels intuition, validates formal market studies, and enhances customer responsiveness. There are four reasons why it works so well:

1. *It provides an unarguable version of the truth for the individuals concerned.* However skewed the sample, views are founded on something seen directly. When the CEO finds that the gas pumps do not work, he is in a position to refute without fear of contradiction that the project manager is wrong when the manager says that the refurbishment has been completed. Of course, if improvement requires heavy investment, you need to do research to check whether a particular incident reflected a systematic problem rather than a one-off glitch. But you usually do not need to do that. Instead, assume that every problem encountered is a potential opportunity for improvement.

2. *Immersion provides a filter through which to view indirect data, such as formal market research.* It helps the management team process data and direct challenges at interpretations of the information that do not fit its own observations in the field. It was not until a member of Hilti's executive board saw with his own eyes the scale of the mining opportunity—something that had previously been identified in the market research and engineering reports—that he championed the idea. He responded personally and with passion to his colleagues' justifiable concerns and, therefore, pushed the initiative through.

3. *It provides an excellent source of storytelling and anecdote.*
   This is crucially important in managing large organizations, where the ability to persuade people to follow can
   hinge upon engaging them emotionally. Tony Pidgley,
   founder and chairman of Berkeley Homes, a builder and
   developer of luxury homes in the United Kingdom, spent
   a week as a foreman on one of his building sites.[10] He was
   particularly disappointed at his company's lax approach
   to customer care. The customer care representative on-
   site did not have a cell phone and was almost impossible
   to reach. His "office" was a run-down storeroom located
   in a remote—and possibly dangerous to visit—location
   on the site. Pidgley found a litany of unanswered complaints from customers who had already moved into their
   new homes. For instance, pillars at the entrances to beau-
   tiful starter mansions oozed with rust because Berkeley
   used the wrong specification of reinforcing steel. Pidgley
   discovered this problem because he hammered into one
   of the pillars and pulled out the component. He produced the bent piece of metal at a management meeting
   the following Monday, described how he found it and
   what its presence meant, and used it as a symbol of poor
   customer care. His message was accepted and understood. Berkeley Homes revisited what customer care
   meant to the company and instituted new guidelines. The
   organization remains a highly regarded builder in the
   United Kingdom today.

4. *It spreads not just the results of learning but also the act of
   learning.* If your boss sees customers one day a week,
   unless you do, too, he or she is going to know more than

you do. In a successful, customer-oriented culture, that means you will not win arguments, and you will not succeed in the organization.

Although we are strong advocates of direct customer contact, it should not be random. Programs should ensure that a good cross-section of executives get exposed to a realistic customer base and should cover all customer groups, all geographic areas, and all functions. Most important, the programs should pay particular attention to *lead users*—those customers who tend to adopt innovations earlier than their competitors. Eric von Hippel and his colleagues at MIT have found compelling evidence that working closely with lead users can give a supplier a competitive advantage through early involvement in new technology and market opportunities.[11]

You should complement direct customer-contact programs with more-formal market studies—especially studies of market needs, usage, attitudes, and customer satisfaction. In addition, fresh insights can emerge from less traditional approaches, such as mystery shoppers (either face-to-face or by phone or e-mail) and ethnography (i.e., participant observation of users in the real-life usage context, perhaps using photography or video).

Understanding Your Competition Because Value Is Relative

Direct customer contact, observation studies, and more traditional customer surveys do not by themselves provide sufficient insight to point the way forward. They must be complemented by a good understanding of the competition. Markets are pretty efficient in the medium and long term. Your good idea this month belongs to the whole world next month or, at best, next year. Competitors are in business because they too have customers who think they are doing a reasonable job. You should never think they are unworthy. Generally, they recruit from the same talent pools, have access to the same factors of production, and buy much the same market research reports as you do. You and your competitors are all in business because you respond to the same market in ways that are broadly similar. By watching your customers and each other and by responding quickly, you collectively nudge quality in the right direction and grow the market. To ensure that you keep pace and understand the customer's shifting perceptions of performance on the basics, you need to be vigilant about your competitors' capabilities and how their efforts to deliver the basics will evolve. To do that, you must try to get inside your competitors' minds.

Getting Inside Your Competitors' Minds

As well as asking the CEOs mentioned earlier in this chapter about their time allocation, we explored some of their other attitudes and practices. The single biggest discriminator between high- and low-performing companies was the extent to which they were sensitive to competitor moves. About two-thirds of respondents from high-performing companies, compared to only a quarter of respondents from the low performers, agreed that "no matter what department they are in, people in this business get recognized for being sensitive to competitive moves."[12]

Follow-up interviews suggest that successful businesses combine formal and informal approaches to understanding their competitors. At each point in time, they focus on just one or two specific themes (e.g., a competitor's pricing policy or recruitment and retention strategy). Teams are formed to model and/or role-play competitors in a given situation, and everyone in the organization is expected to contribute to the learning activity. New insights are shared (e.g., through a "war room"), and exploration, challenge, and even dissent are encouraged. As with customer understanding, the focus of competitor understanding is on insight, not just analysis. In the words of one interviewee: "I don't want to have 'profiles' of my competitors; I want to know how their minds work. I want to know them better than they know themselves."

Knowing how your competitors' minds work can obviously be invaluable. You can better understand their likely next moves, how they would interpret your own planned new moves, and, better still, how they may respond. However, the demand coming down from the executive suite to those charged with this task should be at least a little scary. Imagine it is you who will have to tear yourself away from spreadsheet analysis, poring over company annual reports and media coverage. How on earth will you ever know enough to be able to claim to know how your competitors' minds work? The head of a major global consulting firm summarized his approach as follows:

- *Focus on only a handful of competitors.* There are others and you should not ignore them, but work really hard on just a few.

- *One at a time; go back two years.* Pick up on the half-dozen or so big things they have done. Maybe they have opened a new division or laid off a lot of people in a specific business. Think of these events as critical. Build your interpretation around them.

- *Try to discern the one or two truths that must exist for* all *of these events to have made sense.* Then you are beginning to articulate the underlying strategy.

- *Share this emerging view of the strategy with a few relevant colleagues* who have direct and indirect contact with that competitor. Agree, based on all you can put your hands on, what you believe that strategy is.

- *Share this interpretation of the strategy with all customer-facing staff.* Explicitly ask them to validate it against their experiences in the market.

- *Be prepared to make explicit predictions*—and be prepared to revise them in response to fresh market data and insights.

Activating the Antennae of Every Employee: Hilti's "Competitor Radar"

Hilti implemented a "competitor radar" globally and made each country manager responsible for gleaning from the salesforce any moves by competitors that are outside Hilti's interpretation of their strategy. The company expects country managers to report these gaps to designated competitor experts around the world and disseminates any update widely across the organization. For example, reports originating from technical sales representatives as far apart as Chile, Argentina, France, and Austria gave early warning of two major competitors who were piloting new sales channels. Hilti was able to allocate resources to monitor and evaluate those moves. As a result, discussions about the evolution of Hilti's own channel strategy were informed not only by formal market research but also by the likely evolution of what the competition would be offering.

Hilti's competitor radar has been critical in giving early warning of competitors' new product launches, enabling it to make quick countermoves in selected territories. The real benefit, however, is not in such reactive behavior but rather in forcing product managers out of their comfort zones. One competitor's product introduction was almost ignored by the relevant product management team that had been informed about it after TSs in France and the United States observed on-site customer tests and duly reported them. The product team, probably rightly, felt that the well-established Hilti solution was greatly superior and that the competitor's technology had no future. The team members' reaction was, therefore, confined to sales tactics in the markets concerned. They did not consider the strategic implications of the competitor's action, such as what the second-generation product would look like, when it might arrive, or what the competitor's strategic intent was in introducing the new line.

Hilti's competitor radar aims to force the company to spend time on precisely those types of questions. In this case, however, despite loud protests from TSs in several countries, Hilti's product management team did not stop and review its strategy for product development until it received clear reports from Japan and the United States that the competitor was testing the second-generation product, which customers considered better than the Hilti solution. Hilti then needed urgently to consider the potential impact the new competitor entrant would have, dramatically revise the specification of its own new product development, and plan a product introduction that would trump the competitor.

Competition from Unexpected Sources
As the Source of New Opportunities

Most executives can easily agree with colleagues as to which are their main current competitors. They most often mention the biggest competitors that appear in most customers' consideration sets. Although this makes sense, it overlooks potentially more significant companies currently competing on the periphery. These peripheral competitors often win category share almost unnoticed because they address a largely unrealized, unarticulated market need. They are not even thought of as competitors, but when noticed, they are often admired. We urge executives to temper their admiration with caution. Better to see these players as a potential source of ideas. They can provide helpful early insights on evolving solutions for evolving needs.

Chux pioneered disposable diapers and in doing so provided critical insight to the eventual market leader, Procter & Gamble's Pampers. Micro Instrumentation and Telemetry Systems did the same for IBM and Apple in personal computing. Ampex did it for the Japanese in video recorders. Researchers Peter Golder and Gerard Tellis point out that the principal beneficiaries of these pioneers were the early market leaders who succeeded because they had a vision of the mass market, ample capital, a focus on further improvement, and a broad asset base, including brand equity and extensive operational skills, that they could leverage to achieve market leadership.[13] In our terms, these are typically simply better companies.

Peripheral scanning is a key element of any competitor-monitoring program with an eye to identifying emergent category needs.

Focusing on Where the Whole Category Is Failing to Deliver

You should also ask how you *and* your competitors could improve dramatically. Where do you all fall short? That is, focus on how the whole category could improve. Probe customers for dissatisfaction with the performance of all suppliers combined—not just with your brand versus the competition. This probing can produce remarkable results. It worked for Cemex, the giant Mexican cement producer that grew from a regional player to a world leader by focusing on customers' most basic category needs, not on nice-to-have extras.

Cemex—Differentiating a Commodity Through Better Basics

What are the basics in the supply of ready-mix concrete in trucks with rotating barrels? Think about it from the perspective of the immediate point of contact, the project manager or foreman on a construction site. What does he want from all suppliers? To him, it is crucial to know when cement or other supplies will arrive on-site. Normally, cement ordered the previous day would usually arrive within three hours of the scheduled time, but with no guarantee. Since 1995, Cemex has guaranteed its customers same-day delivery within twenty minutes of schedule in designated geographic markets, regardless of weather conditions, including traffic-jammed Mexico City.[14] For delays, customers receive discounts of about 5 percent. Cemex can make these guarantees because it uses a satellite- and Web-based truck dispatch system to speed and monitor customer deliveries. The system has increased truck productivity by 35 percent. The value to customers is enormous since the process greatly enhances their ability to schedule workflows on-site, leading to much higher total project productivity. Customers buy productivity and assurance embedded in their cement.

The lesson from Cemex is to think through the whole purchase and usage process experienced by the customer. Sometimes the inefficiencies that create the possibility of value enhancement are clear; sometimes an industry colludes unwittingly to make things more difficult than they should be for customers. In some cases even a simple survey can throw up significant opportunities.

A McKinsey study reported that, when asked which of four service improvements were most important to European domestic electricity customers, 41 percent nominated "shorter call center waiting times," 27 percent opted for "more frequent billing," a further 27 percent chose "speedier connection to new property," and only 5 percent requested "a reduction in length of power cuts." Yet the electricity companies' resource allocation, partly in response to regulation, prioritized the latter. Worse, there was little correlation between investments to reduce power cuts and actual performance on this measure. The companies could have simultaneously saved themselves money and increased customer satisfaction by focusing on improving their call centers, their billing systems, and the time they took to connect new properties and by making operational improvements, supported by appropriate new investments, in reducing power cuts.[15]

Daewoo—Asking About Customers' Worst-Ever Experience in the Category

Carmaker Daewoo, before its entry into the highly competitive U.K. auto market, offered yearlong free use of a Daewoo to the hundred applicants with the worst war story of poor service from a garage. The company was amazed to find one hundred twenty-five thousand people applied; that is, one hundred twenty-five thousand people believed that their story might be among the worst one hundred, enough to bother to take the considerable time to apply. This response gave Daewoo publicity, customer insight, and a large database of potential customers. The moral is that customers are often willing to tell you about their experiences—if you ask.

Daewoo sort of stumbled into this situation. When it entered the market in 1995, its challenge was to achieve an unprecedented annual sales target of about eighteen thousand five hundred cars, or 1 percent volume market share, by the end of its third year. Daewoo was completely unknown. When asked who or what Daewoo was, 96 percent of the population had no clue, and 3 of the 4 percent who thought they knew thought that Daewoo was a religion. Learning that Daewoo was a Korean company only raised doubts about quality. While it may have been reassuring to some that the company's two models were based on General Motors designs, those designs were fifteen years old. Despite such challenges, Daewoo not only achieved the objective as stated; it did so after only twelve months. Central to its success was its recognition of the unmet (not latent but unmet) needs of a large segment of the car-buying public.

Daewoo's research had shown that private motorists were most unhappy with their buying and ownership experiences. Eighty-four percent said that the treatment they got from a dealer was as important as how they felt about the car. Fifty-seven percent felt that buying a car was a hassle, and 63 percent found showrooms to be intimidating places where they were subjected to hard-sell tactics. Further, 78 percent said that they were treated even worse after buying a car than before. All these statistics were in the context of a large market segment that was not very interested in cars anyway. A Daewoo study claimed that 37 percent of car buyers regarded their car primarily as a way of just getting from A to B.[16] They were more concerned with the practicalities of car ownership than with car performance, engineering, brand, or esthetics.

Daewoo focused on addressing those unmet needs. By showing that it was serious about delivering on its customer-friendly value proposition, Daewoo persuaded a skeptical public that it would make the process of buying and owning a car stress-free. In achieving its market share objective for year three in just one year, it became the most successful ever car launch in the United Kingdom. Critical to its execution were building the right business system and getting the attention of the mass market, which is understandably skeptical about claims of customer centricity. We return to both those themes later. In addition to learning about exemplary market sensing from Daewoo's U.K. launch team, this case also flags one of the most important points we must insist on. Simply better is a never-ending story. It needs constant attention and dedication to customer value creation. In the case of Daewoo, however, the parent company almost went bankrupt in 2002, which badly undermined the credibility and market position of the U.K. business.[17] Nevertheless, Daewoo's U.K. launch remains an outstanding example of strategy and execution based on customers' dissatisfaction with an established category.

We find that companies with really good customer understanding are often presented with great opportunities for beating their competition—not by developing a USP, but by delivering widely valued generic benefits. Somewhat counterintuitively, they do this by paying uncommon attention to the drivers of *dis*satisfaction.

Hilti and Schindler—Measuring and Monitoring the Drivers of Dissatisfaction

Most companies do try to do better on the things customers say they care about—the drivers of satisfaction. We have found that there is much to learn from paying equal attention to the drivers of dissatisfaction.

Hilti's studies revealed that one major driver of dissatisfaction was imperfection in the fulfillment process. Get fulfillment wrong, and you may have blown the chances of that customer being happy, satisfied, and committed to your brand.

Operationally, Hilti tracks thirty-three components of the four key elements of fulfillment (completeness, on-time shipping, carrier reliability, and credits issued) every month. A sudden drop in the reliability of one of Hilti's carriers triggered one opportunity that came up through such detailed monitoring. On-time delivery fell from 97.5 percent to 93.4 percent in January 2000 for shipments by one of the two courier companies Hilti used in North America. Thousands of customers were understandably irate with Hilti. The company drilled down into its customer activity database and found that the problem came from a major hub used by the courier. As a result, Hilti management met the top management of the courier company to describe the details of the problem, which was affecting both Hilti's and other companies' satisfaction with the courier. The courier immediately instituted corrective action, and, by April 2000, carrier reliability reached 97.7 percent. A win-win.

Managing the drivers of customer satisfaction and dissatisfaction, coupled with top management's commitment to creating fans, or brand advocates, has raised Hilti's overall performance in North America. Top- and bottom-line overall performance in the 1990s was well ahead of most of Hilti's other major markets and the industry, particularly in the latter part of the decade.

Simply focusing on drivers of dissatisfaction can yield substantial gains. Schindler, the $5.5 billion global player in the development, installation, and service of elevators and escalators, provides encouraging evidence. Rick Tower, responsible for supporting quality improvement globally at Schindler, reported that simple focus on "dissatisfiers" drove overall customer ratings in Chile from 2.75 on a 5 point scale in 1998 and 1999 to 4.3 out of 5 by the end of 2000. By 2002, 48 percent of new-installation customers were very satisfied about their installations (up from 7 percent in 1998), and only 2 percent were either dissatisfied or very dissatisfied (down from 30 percent in 1998). Today, Chile's overall customer satisfaction rankings place it in the top-five Schindler operations worldwide in two out of six categories. Schindler Chile was the proud winner of the Ibero-American Quality Award for midsize companies in 2000. Its employee satisfaction statistics place it above the Latin American norm.

Our overall advice is not simply to pick one of the approaches to identify and better understand the basics in your served category; do it all: Ask the customer directly, look to your competitors, and be brutally honest in probing where the category is failing customers.

There is another excellent source of ideas, again from other companies—companies that you do not usually see in your category. Initial reactions to these companies' emergence are often,

"Oh, they have an interesting offer, but it doesn't really compete with us." Sometimes, however, a new category may be being born, possibly one that will dominate you and your competitors before too long.

USPs That Create and Define a Whole New Category

Sometimes, an innovator introduces a new product, service, or business model that really does create its own, defensible market. In some cases the resulting new category is larger than what came before, and the innovator dominates it in the long term, as Canon did with small photocopiers. Encouraged by such success stories, scholars such as Costas Markides and Gary Hamel have argued for radical strategic innovation that breaks the current rules of the game.[18] We urge caution. Both Markides and Hamel represent a special case of our general argument. The companies those scholars describe, such as Southwest Airlines, Starbucks, Dell, CNN, and Wal-Mart, succeeded because they successfully created *new categories* by addressing latent needs and then continued to provide the new generic category benefits, once those emerged, better than the later entrants. Those innovative companies were inspired, and they were lucky. They also had substance, in every case paying great attention to operations and execution.

This type of radical innovation is sometimes called a "flanking strategy," which positions the company on uncontested, virgin territory. The financial rewards are spectacular . . . when the strategy succeeds. History then shows the innovator to have been right: The offering really did tap a large latent need. The company successfully developed the right offering and marketing mix to build and dominate the market and defend it against later entrants who piled in once it became clear that there was a big new market.

Remember, however, that Golder and Tellis have shown that, contrary to popular belief, it is unusual for the innovator to win.[19] Steven P. Schnaars, a marketing guru at Baruch College, has documented many cases of successful imitation strategies.[20] Again and again, once the innovator showed that a new product had a big market potential, others—usually large, established companies with relevant resources and great execution (in our terms, simply better companies)—came in and both drove and dominated the market.

For instance, the first real warehouse clubs were opened by Price Club in 1975. The USP was low, low prices. By 1983 it was clear that many consumers were willing to accept the inconvenience, the Spartan decor, the limited product range, and the cash-only payment rules to save money at Price Club. So the competitors piled in: Sam's Club, Costco, Kmart's Pace. Price Club's total sales grew from $1 billion in 1983 to nearly $30 billion in 1991, but the new entrants were so strong that it was forced to sell out to Costco in June 1993.

Scanning emergent players should be a critical element of better understanding what really matters to customers. Incorporating such scanning makes sense. It acknowledges that markets are dynamic and customer preferences evolve. With that in mind, and armed with fresh ways to think about what really matters to customers, we next turn to making innovation actually happen.

IDEA CHECK

How good are you at sensing what really matters to customers?

1. How much time do you spend directly with customers?

Remember Hilti's fifty-day rule, and forget socializing. Leverage your employees: They spend time with customers, too.

2. Relative to systematic formalized market research, how important are experiences from samples of one in determining strategy?

If your immersion strategy is working, it will offer fresh insight and enrich everything you gain from traditional research.

3. Do you know what your competitors do really well and what they are trying to do better?

You must assess whether you can really predict what your competitors will do next. Have some of your own people conduct a competitor review on your own company.

4. Given the opportunity, what would the market beg you and your competitors to change?

Think through your business system, focus on everything between you and the consumer: distributors, agents, wholesalers, packaging, distribution—everything.

4

Challenges of Innovating
to Drive the Market

Creativity is thinking up new things.
Innovation is doing new things.[1]

—Theodore Levitt,
Edward W. Carter Professor of
Business Administration, Emeritus,
Harvard Business School

Tesco—Relentless Focus on
Customer Value Enhancement

At the beginning of the 1990s, J Sainsbury was the undisputed king of U.K. supermarkets, clearly positioned as the leader in customer service, quality, and innovation. Arch-rival Tesco was losing volume as its core market of price-conscious households felt the onset of the recession and switched to limited-range deep discounters such as Kwik Save, Aldi, and Netto. By the end of the 1990s, Tesco had been transformed. It had increased sales by 250 percent to £18.8 billion, and its market share had reached

16 percent (see figure 4-1). It had a highly successful online operation, Tesco.com, and had enjoyed considerable further success from overseas ventures. Sainsbury lagged on all measures.

So, what happened? Tesco's resurgence came from a combination of expanding into nonfood items, introducing new formats, making some successful acquisitions, and pricing competitively. It positioned itself as a good-value retailer for all shoppers, and it innovated relentlessly. It embraced being better rather than being different. And it particularly focused on being better than leader Sainsbury. Tesco learned from Sainsbury, treated it as a benchmark, and sought to beat it wherever possible. CEO Ian MacLaurin charged one young executive hired in 1979, Terry Leahy, to copy whatever Sainsbury did.[2] That approach was key in the early stages of the turnaround. By the time Leahy was installed as marketing

FIGURE 4-1

Market Share of U.K. Supermarkets

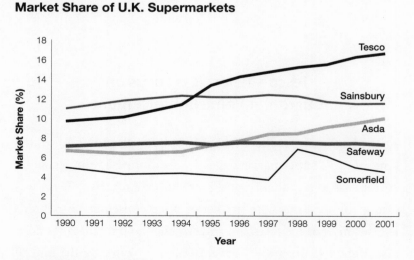

Source: Institute of Grocery Distribution.

director in 1992, he declared it was time to leave Sainsbury behind and focus primarily not on them but on customers. Leahy, with his finely honed competitive instinct and focus on customer value creation, was destined to become CEO, a title he earned in 1997.

Delivering on a Very Wide Range of Dimensions

For supermarkets, delivering what customers really want is something of a nightmare. Shoppers want everything:

- Ambience—Do I like being there?

- Brand—Is it my favorite or least favorite supermarket?

- Checkout lines—Are they quick or slow?

- Features—What additional features, such as a bank, post office, or gas station, does this store have?

- Fresh food—How good is the quality?

- Layout—Can I find what I want quickly and easily?

- Location—How many minutes away is the store?

- Loyalty scheme—Do I get rewarded for loyalty in a way I value?

- Own label—How good is the store's own label?

- Price—How much cheaper are my shopping trips?

- Product range—Are there any unique products, and do they have the products I want?

- Services—How good is it at providing services that help me, such as home delivery?

- Special offers—Are there lots available or only a few?

- Staff—How friendly, helpful, and efficient are they?

Among all these factors, most shoppers rate location, quality, range, staff, and price as most important. The order and weight of these factors vary according to shopper profile or by shopping mission, for example, whether shoppers are buying a few items or making a big grocery trip. In addition, the economic environment influences store choice. During a recession, price becomes more important. One legacy of the recession of the early 1990s is that the emphasis on value remains a high priority, especially when the economic future is uncertain. As recently as 1998, despite excellent U.K. economic conditions, "value for money" was still top of the list in stated reasons for store choice (18 percent of sixty-five hundred households surveyed put it as their number-one criterion) while "low prices" was a bit lower down (13 percent), suggesting that most shoppers were unwilling to trade range, quality, and fresh food for lower prices.[3] To drive value, innovation needs to be comprehensive.

Terry Leahy, the CEO, set the tone:

> *In overall terms, we should aim to be positively classless, the best value, offering the best shopping trip. This will be achieved by having a contemporary business and therefore one that remains relevant by responding to changing needs. We should aim to be the natural choice of the middle market by being relevant to their current needs and serving them better, i.e., customer-focused.*[4]

Tesco was going for the mass market. Knowing that the competition would quickly copy any advantage, it vowed to be first with consumer-focused initiatives. Living up to that vow required not only a superior understanding of the customer but also an outstanding execution of initiatives that responded to consumer needs. Tesco knew that these initiatives were never going to be unique for long, but the speed of delivery and customer-focused execution, together with integrated communications, could create a sustainable competitive advantage. One analyst even noted that "the route that Tesco took to market leadership was open to all and Tesco started from a disadvantaged position."[5]

Serving the Widest Range of Customers

Tesco successfully broadened its brand appeal to higher and lower socioeconomic groups at the same time. It evolved its superstore offering to forty thousand food products as well as to health and beauty products, CDs and videos, clothing, and gasoline.[6] Through relentless innovation, Tesco also managed to achieve simultaneous leadership in price, service, and quality. Its excellence in execution enabled it to offer a combination of competitive price, quality, range, and service all under the same brand name. From a position of price leadership, it came to master the other category benefits effectively. "[Tesco stores] roll a lot more things from the shopping trip into their calculation of value (than just) price + quality equals value."[7]

Recognizing Changing Customer Needs and Evolving

With the saturation of the superstore market, Tesco recognized that further growth had to come from new concepts and alternative means of distribution. It introduced new formats of smaller and midsize city-center stores, Tesco Metro and Tesco Express, respectively. Tesco's range of store formats enabled it to compete in local markets and to attract share from smaller competitors as well as from weaker national chains. It was also the first to launch home delivery and Internet home shopping on a significant scale.

During this period, Sainsbury largely stuck to its narrower definition of the category as mainly food shopping, where it traditionally had a competitive advantage, while largely disregarding nonfood items such as clothing and other household products. It regarded value as unworthy of expensive communication, focusing instead on a more differentiated strategy based on food quality. Meanwhile, Asda focused on price; Safeway concentrated on catering to mothers with children; Iceland specialized in specific food product ranges such as frozen, non-genetically-modified, and organic foods; and Waitrose confirmed its niche position specializing in the upscale shopper. Unlike most of those competitors, Tesco did not try to differentiate itself by segmenting the market and focusing on only one segment. It skillfully managed to combine the generic category benefits of price, quality, range, and service that are attractive to a broad base of customers. Those drivers appeal to all supermarket shoppers, and Tesco has superbly implemented operational programs to deliver those category benefits.

Innovation for innovation's sake is nonsense, but relentless innovation to improve performance on the generic category benefits is an essential element of sustained business success. Having examined earlier how to stay in tune with—or even ahead of—customers' evolving needs in dynamic markets, we now turn to three challenges that need to be addressed to drive the market through innovation: motivating employees, building the right business system, and combining experimentation with clarity.

The Challenge of Motivating Employees

Recent evidence linking customer satisfaction with market capitalization should encourage managers to attack the sources of customer dissatisfaction as well as customer satisfaction with both the brand and the category more vigorously than in the past.[8] The starting point should be the "service-profit chain," which shows the mutually reinforcing relationships among employee morale, customer satisfaction, and profitability.[9] The need to focus on those relationships is even greater when companies choose to prioritize category over brand and basics over USPs. Two related factors are at work.

First, employees of a simply better company cannot brag that it offers something unique. At least in the short term, engaging and motivating them may be harder than it is for employees of a brand differentiator. Although they may well feel proud to work for a company that is best, the company needs to show employees it is the best and that they have a role in making it best—especially when it has just embarked on a change process and anxiety is high due to uncertainty about the future. In turning around Tesco, Terry Leahy received input from small groups of employees. Their goodwill and enhanced productivity were critical. They were energized when treated with respect and given meaningful work and training. They wanted to enjoy being at work. The role of middle management was also critical. All managers were trained to run meetings effectively, identify the causes of a problem, spot resistance to change, and do something about it.[10]

It is important that this attention to human relations is not fleeting. Tesco has embedded teamwork, praise, and trust into its core values and continues to listen hard to all employees. It now has an employee insight unit. All staff are surveyed annually, and smaller sample surveys are conducted every six months. Suggestions arising from staff feedback have yielded about $15 million in direct annual savings. Extending the concept of immersion to employee contact, Tesco launched Tesco Week in the Store Together (TWIST). Among the thousand head office managers to go through the program along with Leahy was Claire Chapman, the human resources director. For Chapman, the big lesson from TWIST was the importance of keeping life simple for staff.[11]

Second, employees need to understand their personal role in customer value creation, especially if the strategy is changing. In retailing and other mass consumer services, the salesforce includes all direct customer-contact staff—often the most powerful communication medium of all. Similarly, in professional services such as management consulting, anyone who has direct customer contact is part of both the product and the communication about that product. Monitoring and enhancing employee morale and leveraging the opportunities presented by direct customer contact are critical if you are to be simply better.

Measuring Employee Morale at Hilti

In the early 1990s Hilti began to measure employee morale. The company had learned how critical it was that all employees had a good sense of the organization's direction. With the implementation of a new strategy, Champion 3C, the executive board started to devote more time and attention to ensuring that all employees understood and supported the new strategy that would focus on three core elements: knowing the *customer*, developing specific *competencies* required to execute, and *concentrating* resources on key areas and strategic new opportunities.[12] The data it collected from a rolling survey covering every employee every two years was used for operational improvement within each country, business unit, and headquarters function. Additionally, the executive board gained three powerful new insights:

1. The first is an extension of the service-profit chain. Hilti's analysis found strong, positive correlations between employee morale, the percentage of customers who were Hilti fans, and profit.

2. A key driver of employee morale at every level was the confidence and respect employees had for their immediate bosses.

3. Employees who reported high satisfaction also said that they understood the Champion 3C strategy.

At a broader level, the executive board believed that employees must see senior management walk the talk of the new strategy. In 1993, when employees in several of the larger Hilti markets were surveyed, it became clear that they had little understanding of Strategy 2000, the precursor to Champion 3C.[13] Consequently, the company strove to communicate the new strategy and its implementation. When it launched Champion 3C, Hilti management presented and discussed it with all fourteen thousand employees in some two thousand small half-day workshops.

What is interesting is not that Hilti collects the data to facilitate operational improvement but rather the extent to which executive board members get their hands dirty with the data.

They seek to explain not only movements and trends but also themes and relationships. On one occasion, when CEO Pius Baschera confirmed his expectation that the positive relationship between employee morale, perceived service quality, customer satisfaction, and profitability of a business found in cross company research would be found also when the only data examined were from Hilti's own operations, his instinct led him to dig deeper. Would the same effects be observed if you separated out front- and back-office employees? Further analysis revealed a strong positive correlation between morale among non-customer-facing employees and fans—something of particular interest in an organization where almost two-thirds of all employees are customer-facing and back-office people might be seen as only loosely connected to customer satisfaction.

Executives must go beyond the headline findings. Material movements in employee morale may happen long before the results of a periodic study. Measurement can be used both as a steering tool and for coaching smaller groups. It is easier to do that when you know the overall level of morale across business units and morale trends. You must also be able to contextualize the data. For example, you might find that a group of employees was surveyed immediately before the appointment of a new general manager, which might have created momentary uncertainty and decreased the underlying morale level.

Monitoring the Energy Level

It is important when striving to be better rather than different that employees not get demoralized in the face of short-term competitive challenges. A Michigan-based consulting firm called eePulse has developed a simple system that "takes the pulse" of a business and tracks it. The pulse is the energy level of an individual employee, a team, a department, or a whole business. Employees take their own pulse every week by assessing their energy level. They receive structured feedback that allows them to assess their pulse relative to their self-defined target zone, other members of their team, and the business as a whole. The target zone is the area that they feel they need to be in to be effective. It depends on whether the employee is in sales, analysis, administration, and so on. Companies such as General Motors, RR Donnelley, and Oxygen Media have all used this real-time method of tracking employee morale.

Leveraging Frontline Contact

High-ticket B2B categories such as capital goods rely mainly on the salesforce as a direct communication channel with customer organizations. Frequently purchased items sold through third-party distribution channels such as supermarkets use the salesforce mainly for communicating with the trade. Increasingly, as the retail trade becomes more concentrated, the number of low-level field salespeople shrinks, being partly replaced by an internal telephone salesforce and Internet communications. At the same time, emphasis on the key account teams that work as closely as possible with the company's main trade partners increases. In this sense, consumer markets have become more like industrial markets: The relationship between Procter & Gamble and Wal-Mart is not so very different from that between DuPont and General Motors.

Nowadays the front line is increasingly being explicitly integrated into the fundamental offer. At companies such as IBM the salesforce has always been highly knowledgeable about applications and there to offer advice and support to customer staff. Similarly, the Hilti TS is inseparable from the physical product; the company is in the business of selling solutions, not products. The same is true at Medtronic, world leader in pace-makers and other implantable medical devices, which sells through its field force of specialists who work alongside cardiac surgeons in the operating theater as members of the surgical team. According to Bill George, former CEO and chairman, many surgeons will not start a procedure until the specialist from Medtronic has arrived, scrubbed up, and is standing at the surgeon's side.[14]

Building the Right Business System

All successful organizations do and should try to drive the market. In innovating we caution against compromise. Protect the business system that delivers customer value according to plan. In principle, the approach is easy to state. First, achieve complete clarity on the customer value proposition to the served market. Once you obtain that clarity, design a business system that delivers the value proposition to the highest level. In practice, however, difficult trade-offs are inherent: low cost versus high quality versus fast response, productivity versus flexibility and wide range, efficiency versus customization. Although new technology, especially IT, is pushing back many of those boundaries, trade-offs are part and parcel of being simply better. Having a clear sense of the fundamental proposition, that is, knowing which basics the customer really wants, should guide this process.

Ryanair—Achieving Clarity on the Customer Value Proposition

Earlier, we set out some simple yet often overlooked approaches to understanding what customers really want. These apply also when it comes to articulating your value proposition in a way that allows innovation to focus on improving how customer value is created. To understand what customers really want, first spend time directly with them, give them a channel to gripe, and listen intently. Then look at the drivers of dissatisfaction. A need is always unmet when customers tell you they are disappointed. For the seller, failing to meet needs you set out to satisfy is the worst kind of unmet need. Assume that, whatever need you are trying to satisfy, not doing so renders it unmet.

It is amazing to hear executives tell us of their attempts to think outside the box when their businesses still suffer from abysmal satisfaction ratings. It is a little like a weekend golfer who routinely loses five balls in the rough on every round and worries about how to get more backspin on his chip. Instead, you should first work hard to pick up any evidence of dissatisfaction—the equivalent of following through with your swing. Understand the most important category benefits, and prioritize fixing those over heroic schemes to rewrite the rules of the game or reinvent the business model. But do not be complacent. Budget airlines continue to teach national carriers important lessons about giving customers what they want. Although it is tempting to think of them as rule breakers, they are not really. They developed a valid business model to deliver a lot of customer value, and they do not rest on their laurels—they continue to drive the market. In Europe, the star budget airline is Ryanair.

Immediately prior to its acquisition of Go in 2002, easyJet was valued at $1.7 billion. Meanwhile Ryanair, with a market capitalization of $6.5 billion, had surpassed national carriers such as Lufthansa and British Airways to become the most valuable airline in Europe. It would be a mistake to attribute Ryanair's success simply to bringing new low-income travelers into the market. An independent study in July 2002 by consultants Simon-Kucher & Partners of travelers from a German airport served by Ryanair reported that the customers were young (38 percent were between ages 25 and 34, 21 percent between 35 and 44); more than half had university degrees; they were likely to have above-average incomes; two-thirds had traveled on business in the past two years; and one quarter had traveled on more than twelve round-trips for business purposes.[15] Budget airlines have mass-market appeal because they address unmet, or poorly met, basic needs for cheap, simple air travel. Forty percent of Southwest Airlines's passengers come from the business community, the frequent fliers who seek cheap, simple air travel from point A to point B.

Combining low fares with good customer service can be compelling if well enough executed. JetBlue has focused on service, actively cultivated loyalty, and benefited from the positive word of mouth associated with good customer experiences. In the words of CEO Dave Neeleman, the company "brings humanity back to air travel."[16] With this formula JetBlue has achieved darling status on Wall Street and with customers. It had the second lowest (after Southwest Airlines) rate of customer complaints registered at the U.S. Department of Transportation.[17] Not even four years old, JetBlue's market capitalization has reached $3.6 billion.

Ryanair's model is different. By offering only the scantest service, Ryanair attracts legions of customer complaints. Some wags even call it Eireoflot, a take on the notoriously bad customer service on Soviet-era Aeroflot flights. How could such a service be customer-focused? Is it not simply an example of operational excellence? A headline from a British newspaper reveals a clue: "It's the World's Worst Airline. And I Love It."[18] In that article columnist Simon Calder comments that, although Ryanair infuriates customers, they will buy again. They will take a gamble. If a delay occurs, Ryanair will not provide food or accommodation. In the eyes of CEO Michael O'Leary, there is simply no problem:

> Our customer service proposition is about the most well defined in the world. We guarantee to give you the lowest airfare. You get a safe flight. You get a normally on-time flight. That's the package. We don't and won't give you anything more on top of that. . . . We care for our customers in the most fundamental way possible: we don't screw them every time they fly.[19]

O'Leary is utterly focused on delivering his value proposition. He does not panic when he hears his airline is one of the most complained about. He knows that some dissatisfaction exists, and if he followed our advice blindly, he would do something about it. The lesson is not obvious. Ryanair does not get complaints about failing to deliver on its actual value proposition. Some travelers are upset because they perceive that the company fails to deliver on what they imagine the value proposition *should be*. O'Leary, on the other hand, focuses on what it is and keeps pushing the limits on it. He recently articulated a future vision of air travel totally free of charge to the traveler. Likening his business to network TV, which delivers eyeballs to advertisers, he hopes that one day Ryanair will be paid by city authorities eager to benefit from the economic activity generated by travelers landing at their airport rather than that of another city in the region.[20]

Progressive—Combining Experimentation with Clarity

Experimentation is an attractive approach. It has been credited with giving companies such as British Petroleum, Banc One, and General Motors valuable insights on how to deliver greater customer value.[21] The challenges here are to ensure that you do not just experiment for the sake of it and to know when and how to decide that the experiment is over and you will need to try something else. Consider Progressive Insurance, an avid experimenter, innovator, and killer of dud projects.

Progressive designed a business system that enabled it to make money from insuring "high-risk," or more politely "nonstandard," automobile drivers. That system then turned out to deliver a value proposition with mass-market appeal. With a strong emphasis on execution, Progressive has grown to be the fourth largest auto insurer in the United States.

Progressive first recognized the nonstandard segment—20 percent of all motorists—in 1956. It set about creating a business system that would enable it to make money where others had failed. Nonstandard drivers were those thought more likely to have an accident and make a claim. Typically, they had a poor safety record, did not speak English as a first language, drove high-performance vehicles, or were either over sixty-five years old or young first-time drivers with no record. For insurers, it was harder to make money from nonstandard drivers because experience showed that they generated above-average costs. Additionally, nonstandard drivers were more likely to miss payments, relocate, or cancel policies. In contrast to a standard driver, who seldom if ever lets the policy lapse, the average policy duration for nonstandard drivers was only eighteen months.

Progressive's Business System

The characteristics of nonstandard drivers made selling them insurance superficially unattractive. But Progressive saw them as an opportunity and fashioned an integrated business system that enabled it to do business with them profitably. The main features were:

- Investing in error-free data capture, information systems, analytical tools, and underwriting, enabling Progressive to assess and price risk better than the competition. Progressive was hailed as the "Prince of Smart Pricing."[22]

- Double-checking policies. Savings in reducing bad pricing more than offset the additional costs.

- Introducing a fast comparative-quotation service that offered customers quotes from Progressive and estimations of quotes from competitors. Frequently its own price was not the lowest.

- Investing in claims handling. Since both fraud and lawyer involvement were big cost drivers (fraud alone added

10 percent to 15 percent to estimated insurance losses), it was critical to get a loss adjuster on to the case, usually within hours. This meant having adjusters on call 24/7 and giving policyholders toll-free numbers to call. Often claims were settled at the scene of the accident.

- Incentivizing business managers to achieve a 4 percent profit target from underwriting. When a manager's under-writing profit dropped from 5 percent to 4 percent, the incentive element of his or her compensation went down by about 8 percent. But, if profit dropped to 3 percent, the incentive went down 40 percent.

Progressive had tuned its business system to meet the needs of "difficult" customers. It delivered good prices transparently and with very quick settlement. Standard customers began to find that combination attractive. Progressive started actively promoting its ability to deliver on these basic items—basic for any customer. Its 1997 annual report proclaimed that it was in the business of "reducing the human trauma and economic costs of auto accidents, theft, and other perils while building a trusted, admired, business-generating consumer brand."[23] There was no mention of being a specialist nonstandard insurance provider. This evolution happened because innovation had continuously pushed the limits without compromising the business system.

Experimenting While Protecting the Business System

CEO Peter Lewis says that his father, who founded Progressive, was obsessed with allowing executives "the freedom to experiment, to figure out how [we could become better]."[24] Further, it was Lewis's view that anything Progressive did had to be good for the consumer or else there was no point in doing it. This attitude and determination enabled Progressive to introduce technologies, overcome the skepticism of its managers and staff, and become more responsive. It led to the introduction of an automatic quotation system, one of the first in the industry. Initially the system was accessed by telephone, then also via the Web. That system was a successful continuation of Lewis's pushing the limits.

Several less successful experiments followed. Autograph was an adaptation of GPS technology that allowed Progressive to price premiums based on the amount, location, and timing of car use. It considered the actual number of miles a car was driven, where it was driven and parked, and at what times of day it was driven. In 2000 a limited test market in Houston, Texas, produced encouraging results, and with minor adjustments the product was available statewide in 2001. Although the experiment showed the offer's technical feasibility and customer acceptance, it was deemed it to be ahead of its time. Citing technical barriers and business system complexity (Progressive would have to rely on a third-party technology provider) the company discontinued Autograph in late 2001.[25]

Similarly, after a rolling pilot in four states starting in Arizona in March 2000, Progressive discontinued its home insurance experiment. Like other insurers, Progressive had become interested in cross-selling existing customers. Through pilot tests, it learned that required adjustments to its business system would have compromised its standards. In particular, offering home insurance would have risked one of the competitive advantages the company had carefully developed—its smooth interaction with independent agents. Home insurance would have required those agents to do a lot more work before signing a client and to visit more homes than in the auto market.

Clearly, Progressive wants to protect and adhere to its business system. It conducts business in a certain way for which it expects a specific return. Many standard drivers are willing to pay extra to allow them to deal with an insurance company which they see as fair and open. Progressive did not have to adjust its business system much to attract them. Our point here is that the Progressive success story is often erroneously understood as a victory of market segmentation. In fact, we think it is unhelpful to think of what Progressive did over the long term as specializing in nonstandard drivers. Instead, it assessed and priced risk at the level of the individual; it focused on execution and on delivering on the basics better than the competition. Its value proposition is attractive to all types of driver willing to pay a bit more for service quality.

Progressive's approach is not as unusual as it may seem. Tesco is simultaneously a mass-market player with a consistent value proposition to all and a world-class one-to-one marketer. Toyota, on the other hand, has one mass-market proposition that it effectively translates into distinct product offerings for different socioeconomic groups, including buyers of luxury cars through Lexus. Although readers of this book may not know about Hilti, there is almost total awareness and understanding of its high-end quality proposition in its served market—professional users. It now also serves independent tradespeople through shop-in-shop outlets in Home Depot and La Plateforme stores. Doing this was a channel management decision. Although Hilti's expanded distribution opens the possibility that do-it-yourself enthusiasts wanting the best will opt for a Hilti power drill, the company's offer remains consistent. In the same way that Joe enthusiast can buy a Hilti if he really wants to, royalty can travel on Ryanair if they wish. Neither the offer nor the terms and conditions change.

Using the Internet to Be Simply Better

Radical thinking and pushing the limits are great in the right context. In golf, backspin is good; straight is better. As a rule, we would be worried if executives were spending more than 10 percent of their time dreaming up the next breakthrough. Further, we believe that one way to think about getting the most out of that 10 percent is to spend much of it scanning new entrants, especially those smaller companies that, not burdened with thinking about your market the way you have for decades, seem to be making something of an impact, gaining attention and customer acceptance. As we have seen, in reality it is the alert, well-capitalized, simply better second movers, not the real pioneers, that usually capture most value from such radical innovations. Finally, while we acknowledge the success of some such flanking strategies, we are loath to recommend flanking as a *normal* growth strategy.

The Internet provides many examples of businesses using technology to be simply better—and quite a few of companies falling in love with technology and forgetting about customers' real needs.

Writing in 2004, it is no longer controversial that many of the failed dotcoms were based on business models that could never work because the value proposition made no sense to customers. In contrast, a few well-known Internet start-ups have survived to create strong brands and viable businesses. Examples include eBay, Amazon.com, Yahoo!, and Google. All of them combine a service that meets real customer needs (e.g., reduced search costs) with outstanding execution and attention to the basics. For instance, Amazon is so good at logistics that Toys 'R Us, having failed to deliver toys in time for Christmas 1999, went to the Web retailer for online ordering and fulfillment functionality.[26]

Most successful use of the Internet, however, is by established companies using it to be simply better, mainly through improved customer service and internal and value chain efficiencies. In the early days, companies mainly emphasized direct e-commerce, often trying to cut out a middleman, a process called "disintermediation." For instance, companies such as Saturn, Reebok, Levi Strauss, and A.B.Dick, a maker of printing press equipment, tried to sell direct, in some cases using mass customization to tailor their products for individual customers. These efforts usually proved to be uneconomical as well as to have created conflict with existing channels. Most have been abandoned or drastically scaled back. Of course, e-commerce is growing but usually as a supplement to existing channels. Most of the biggest e-commerce success stories are about companies such as Dell, Ryanair, easyJet, and Tesco.com, who were already selling direct using traditional channels, including the telephone or brick-and-mortar stores.[27]

Today, most companies with established channels use the Internet not to bypass those other channels but instead to strengthen relationships with them, as well as with suppliers and final customers. For instance, Saturn has a program to help its dealers—some of which were still not using e-mail in late 2002—to use technology to improve their customer service and communications. Reebok has developed e-commerce microsites in partnership with key retailers to sell products distributed exclusively through those retailers. A.B.Dick has focused on closely integrating its dealers into its marketing and distribution system.

Consider specialty chemicals producer Eastman Chemical Company. Its Internet programs include the following:

- PaintandCoatings.com, a portal that provides value-added information to users of coating products

- The Chemical Industry Data Exchange, a collaboration among two dozen top chemical companies that has standardized the formats for transferring data electronically between organizations

- Eastman.com, a real-time global interface for 24/7 customer service

With all those initiatives, the acid test could not be simpler: Do they enable the company to improve its offering to customers, either directly (e.g., via better customer service) or indirectly (e.g., via lower costs that lead to lower prices)? The great majority of these successful Internet applications are about generic category benefits. Invariably, they come from careful, step-by-step implementation with enormous attention to detail.

If the product itself is information, especially high-value information that is either very time sensitive (e.g., Reuters or

Bloomberg) or comprises large archives (e.g., LexisNexis), the Internet can obviously provide big category benefits. But as we saw earlier, even cement manufacturer Cemex has used digital technology extensively to deliver the basics better than its competitors. Of course, much nonsense was said and written during the Internet bubble, but that should not blind us to the quiet revolution whereby companies in every industry are steadily incorporating digital technology into their everyday processes and communications to become simply better.

Tesco again offers an interesting example. It never forgot that above all it was a grocer, and that for shoppers the basics remain pretty much the same irrespective of the channel. It certainly did not radically rethink the business the way others, such as Webvan, tried to do. But in just three years, Tesco.com's home-delivery service had grown to cover 95 percent of the United Kingdom. Receiving seventy thousand orders each week and with annual sales of more than £300 million, it accounts for about 10 percent of all online retail commerce in the United Kingdom. Starting in 1996, six junior managers were asked to develop a proposal for a model for home delivery via the Internet. They were given no money, just told to design the model for the new business as they though best. Deliveries were tested from a single store in West London that same year, and the service was tweaked until December 1999, when it started a progressive national rollout. Tweaking based on input from users, such as Lynne Pullam, was extensive.

Lynne Pullam, an Internet consultant for Tesco.com, and people like her provide critical input for what the site looks like. She is not what you would typically think of as an Internet consultant. To Pullam:

A megabyte is a very large mouthful of food, and a hard drive is any journey on the [commuter train] at rush hour. I'm told some people use these terms to describe computers. . . . I may not be technically minded but with 30 years of shopping experience buying food for a hungry family, I can certainly tell Tesco whether shopping on the Internet is easy or not.[28]

John Browett, CEO of Tesco.com, points to Pullam's experience as a customer:

Her experience as a busy mother of three is as valuable to us as an Oxbridge degree in computer science. If Lynne says "No," Tesco won't go. She represents the voice of the customer. . . . The majority of customers using online shopping know little about computer technology. For them it is just a different, more convenient way of doing shopping.[29]

Tesco believes that, compared to others in the Internet space, it took its time, although that is a relative term. Tesco.com still achieved early-mover advantage, something that clearly is not attributable to speed alone. In the words of Browett: "First mover advantage has two parts to it; being first and getting it right. There are loads of examples where people forget the second bit."[30] Tesco's focus on implementation was the key element enabling it to leverage its capabilities and present an offer to customers it knew in a totally fresh way. This kind of rigor in the face of emerging opportunities emanates from an organizational culture that celebrates simplicity and customer focus.

IDEA CHECK

Are you driving the market?

1. Do you have an innovation barometer?

No? Good, no need. Keep focused on measuring whether you are creating real value for real customers today. Understand that customer expectations evolve, and you need to continually push the boundaries.

2. Have you banned thinking outside the box?

You should. It is not the same as innovation. It is too often an excuse for sloppy thinking. Have would-be rule breakers examine their own areas of responsibility. Are they delivering as they should? Quantum leaps are OK only if they're in the right direction.

3. Do your people have faith in their bosses?

They need to. Being better not different requires resolve and belief. It is a prerequisite for enabling them to think through how they can raise the game for the customer.

5

Caution: Inside-the-Box
Advertising Doesn't Work

If you don't get noticed, you don't have anything.
You just have to be noticed, but the art is in getting noticed
naturally, without screaming or without tricks.[1]

—Leo Burnett,
founder of the Leo Burnett Company

Target Corporation—Differentiation That Matters and Advertising That Works

In 2002 the Minneapolis-based Target Corporation leapfrogged Kmart to become the United States's second-biggest discounter behind the $218 billion giant Wal-Mart. According to the *New York Times,* every successful step that Target took brought it into closer confrontation with the formidable leader of the $430 billion general merchandise store industry.[2] Even with sales topping $40 billion in 2002, Target could not achieve the same economies of scale as Wal-Mart. Still, the company was performing spectacularly well. Revenues had grown about 6 percent per year over the previous ten years, and Target had just posted a record operating profit margin of 8.4 percent in 2002 versus Wal-Mart's 7.6 percent. Target was carrying the same categories as Wal-Mart and Kmart. Despite its smaller size, it was able to thrive and coexist profitably with Wal-Mart while Kmart hobbled toward bankruptcy. Target's success was attributable to two key factors: the right kind of differentiation and distinctive marketing communications.

An early strategic choice to build a brand around the Target name fostered the company's steady growth. Gerald Storch, Target's vice chairman, explained that the company had faced three strategic choices to tackle the increased competition in the retail market: "to specialize, to become the low-cost producer, or to differentiate [itself]."[3] The first choice would have thwarted future growth, and Wal-Mart was already a low-cost producer, so Target chose the third option and decided to reposition itself as a mass merchandiser of affordable chic goods.

Achieving the Right Kind of Differentiation

In retailing, the brand is the full experience plus value for money. Great advertising might get shoppers into the store once—but only once if the experience and value for money do not meet expectations. Target avoided competing against Wal-Mart head-to-head and was perceived as outperforming it on specific dimensions: cleanliness of stores, shopping environment and experience, and shorter waiting time to pay (see figure 5-1). Those criteria must have been important to all shoppers, espe-

FIGURE 5-1

Customer Perceptions, Target Versus Wal-Mart

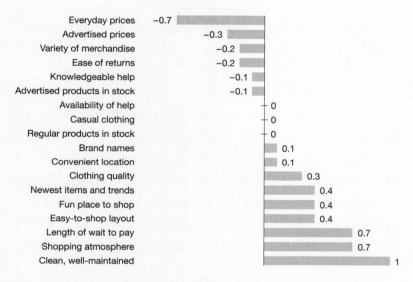

Everyday prices	−0.7
Advertised prices	−0.3
Variety of merchandise	−0.2
Ease of returns	−0.2
Knowledgeable help	−0.1
Advertised products in stock	−0.1
Availability of help	0
Casual clothing	0
Regular products in stock	0
Brand names	0.1
Convenient location	0.1
Clothing quality	0.3
Newest items and trends	0.4
Fun place to shop	0.4
Easy-to-shop layout	0.4
Length of wait to pay	0.7
Shopping atmosphere	0.7
Clean, well-maintained	1

Source: Robert S. Drbul, "Target Corporation: Review of Retail Seminar Presentation" (Lehman Brothers, 7 May 2003).

cially those for whom price was not everything. It is hard to believe Wal-Mart did not also pay attention to those factors.

Interestingly, despite Target's dedication to match Wal-Mart's prices on like items, the company was still perceived as weaker on both everyday prices and advertised prices, as well as on variety of merchandise.[4] Evidently, those perceptions have not held Target back. It has built a very attractive clientele. Compared with those of other discounters, Target's customers, referred to as "guests," are on average younger, better educated, and more affluent. The company has successfully associated its name with a younger, hipper, edgier, and more fun image than its competitors. Target is often pronounced in faux French, "Tar-zhay," to connote its trendy sensibility. To understand how Target has achieved that reputation, we need to examine its successful branding activities.

Successful Design Partnerships and Clever Advertising

Target's business objective was to create an alternative to Wal-Mart's price leadership. It planned do so through upscale discounting, a concept associating style, quality of products, and price competitiveness. This "cheap-chic" strategy enabled Target to become a major brand and consumer-shopping destination, articulated around two main interrelated branding activities: designer partnerships and clever, creative advertising.

Target entered high-profile design partnerships across merchandise lines, from apparel to kitchenware to food. In apparel, it partnered with Mossimo and Isaac Mizrahi and launched new lines that complemented its own private labels, such as Cherokee, Merona, and Xhilaration. Each brand has a specific positioning so that Target's overall assortment appeals to a broad customer base. Target's home assortment also includes brands created by famous designers that are available only in its stores. Philippe Starck's Starck Reality line was introduced in May 2002, followed by Michael Grave's Design assortment, which includes home and office decor products. Recently, in partnership with chef Ming Tsai, Target introduced Blue Ginger, a line of original food products combining Western dishes with a hint of Asian flavors.

Although many retailers have design partnerships, each partnership is unique. With a few exceptions, what matters is not that you have some exclusives with specific designers, but rather how you exploit them. For Target, its design partnerships provided a theme for its advertising, creating synergy between the two main strands of its branding: design and advertising.

Wal-Mart spends 0.3 percent of its revenue on advertising. Target spends 2.3 percent. With the help of more than half a dozen agencies, it regularly comes up with innovative ad campaigns—a singular strategy for a discount store. Through consistent marketing and communication, Target has transformed its signature bull's-eye logo into a lifestyle symbol. The bull's-eye is recognized by 96 percent of American consumers and considered a brand icon in a class with Nike's swoosh and McDonald's arches.[5]

In 1997 Target ran a twelve-month national campaign in unusual spots: the Sunday magazines of the *New York Times, Los Angeles Times,* and *Chicago Tribune,* among others. Ads could also be seen on walls of buildings in New York and in bus shelters from Miami to Philadelphia.[6] One showed a woman riding a vacuum cleaner through the night sky. Another featured a fashionably dressed woman holding a waffle iron with which she had apparently crimped her hair. Both ads used the tagline "Fashion and housewares" in the lower right corner.

More recently, the "bull's-eye world" spots, displaying a funky retro pop culture place where happy blondes serve red bull's-eye-shaped Jell-O molds, was awarded the Marketer of the Year award by *Advertising Age* nineteen years after Wal-Mart won.[7]

Target has also engaged in "dimensional advertising," using unconventional marketing programs to reinforce its message. In 1998 it launched a bridal registry program, Club Wedd. The registry quickly became the largest in the world, surpassing Macy's long-established program and confirming Target's upscale positioning relative to Wal-Mart and Kmart. Other successful programs include:

- Sponsorship of the restoration of the Washington monument

- Take Care of Education program

- Partnership with Coca-Cola in the Color My World red line campaign

- Sponsorship of the CBS program *Survivor*

The success of Target illustrates the importance of distinctive communications in achieving long-lasting differentiation on anything other than price. Target is still a mass merchandiser, providing category basics such as low prices, comprehensive assortment, and shopping convenience. It is not a niche brand, but, through its commitment to design and innovative marketing communications, it has managed to depart sufficiently from Wal-Mart in terms of image and branding to build loyalty among a large and attractive segment of the American population and to grow its business extremely profitably.

The Role of Marketing Communications

Target is a typical successful company in the sense that the main basis of its success is the quality, value for money, and reliability of its offering, but it also excels at marketing communications. Tesco is somewhat similar. The foundation of Tesco's success is great execution and attention to detail combined with relentless customer-focused innovation. But Tesco is also an outstanding database marketer and has won awards for its media advertising, too. In contrast, Wal-Mart, as we have seen, puts little emphasis on communications, relying instead on its low prices and wide product range.

Except for some price leaders like Wal-Mart, marketing communications have an important role, telling the market about product benefits and innovations, increasing the brand salience, reinforcing brand equity, and sometimes generating a direct response, such as a store visit, information request, or actual purchase. Marketing communications' exact role depends on the context, but the challenge of getting them noticed is universal.

In this chapter, we focus mainly on media advertising, the most conspicuous and heavily researched marketing communications activity. The argument, however, applies almost equally to direct marketing, PR, sponsorship, sales promotion, and interactive marketing. In fact, those areas, especially direct and interactive marketing, are gradually becoming more important while traditional media advertising is attracting a slowly declining proportion of total marketing expenditure.[8] These changes in the range and mix of communication channels, if anything, increase the challenge of attracting the attention of customers and prospects. This chapter is about how to meet this growing challenge.

In this book, we argue that simply better businesses differentiate themselves by providing the generic category benefits better than the competition, rather than by providing USPs that the competitors do not provide. We urge managers to forget outside-the-box thinking, at least until their inside-the-box thinking and execution have reached the stage where they are beating the competition on the basics.

In marketing communications, however, inside-the-box thinking by itself will not work. The reason is simple: In today's society, customers receive so many commercial and other messages that they filter out the vast majority, both through selective attention and by using their TV remotes, PC and cell-phone delete buttons, and so on. In order to cut through the clutter and attract the customer's attention, a message needs to be distinctive and eye- or ear-catching, as well as relevant. It requires outside-the-box thinking to develop this kind of message.

Your Product Does Not Need to Be Distinctive but Your Advertising Does

In the rest of this chapter, we look more closely at the USP concept, arguing that the mistake that people have made is to assume that the genuine need for distinctive communications also means that the brand itself needs to be distinctive. We then argue that the key concept for communications development is disciplined creativity. We describe a simple five-step process to achieve such disciplined creativity, illustrated by an example, Land Rover in the United Kingdom.

One key feature of the process is that it starts and ends with disciplined inside-the-box thinking, typically within the client, but allows space for the creative team, typically within an ad agency, to generate outside-the-box ideas in between. In particular, it is important that the communications brief should not constrain *how* the creative strategy will meet its objectives. We illustrate that by contrasting a U.K. government campaign for reading and literacy, which worked only because the ad agency disregarded one of the constraints in the brief, and the Orange launch, where the brief gave the agency wide scope for creative thinking.

We briefly review the need to reassert discipline after a campaign in order to evaluate and learn from the results. Finally, we argue for a sense of perspective about marketing communications, whose role is almost always secondary to that of the product or service and the way it is priced and distributed relative to the competition's.

Generic Category Benefits Versus USPs

Unlike other writers, we believe that most successful differentiation is what we have called the right kind of differentiation: it focuses on what customers really want, rather than on a USP, that is, a specific benefit that only that brand provides. Customers do not expect miracles, just a good deal that provides the best bundle of generic category benefits for their particular need at a reasonable price.

Target is a case in point. That company matches Wal-Mart's prices on items they both sell—which requires an extremely tightly run operation—but certainly cannot claim that its prices are uniquely low. Nor can it claim to be the most chic store in the United States. It does, however, excel relative to Wal-Mart on many aspects of the shopping experience that matter to many consumers. Crucial to its success, Target has found a particular mix of these generic category benefits that appeals to a large and valuable group of the U.S. public. Target's strategy is extremely logical. It did not emerge from wild out-of-the-box thinking about the industry. Its value creation comes instead from its outstanding execution both in operating terms and in terms of great branding and communication.

The USP: What Rosser Reeves Actually Wrote

Although marketers often use the term *unique selling proposition* or *USP,* they tend to do so rather loosely. Rosser Reeves, the advertising man who first coined the term in 1960, gave it a precise three-part definition:[9]

1. Each advertisement must make a proposition to the consumer—not just words, not just product puffery, not just show-window advertising. Each advertisement must say to each reader: "Buy this product, and you will get this specific benefit."

2. The proposition must be one that the competition either cannot or does not offer. It must be unique—either a uniqueness of the brand or a claim not otherwise made in that particular field of advertising.

3. The proposition must be so strong that it can move the mass millions (i.e., to pull over new customers to your product).

This definition is based on three assumptions:

- First, the company can give the brand (through product innovation, etc.) some feature, or features, that *provide a benefit that no other brand provides*—the USP. The role of advertising—Reeves's primary focus—is to communicate that USP single-mindedly and persistently.

- Second, *customers find the USP so compelling that they buy the brand in large numbers* and/or at a premium price.

- Third, *the USP is a source of sustainable competitive advantage.* This assumes that competitors are unable to match it through imitation or that if they do so, the first mover's advertising is so powerful that customers will continue to perceive the benefit as unique even when it no longer is.

Coming up with unique features and benefits is not hard, but coming up with a unique feature or benefit that also meets the second and third conditions is almost impossible because most unique features, such as "the only triangular tea bag," are seen by customers as unimportant. Many of the sillier dotcoms were based on unique benefits no one wanted, such as the ability to buy all your pet food online.

Distinguishing the Brand
from the Advertising About It

Of course, marketing communications and advertising in particular are easier if you have a USP. Advertising people often start by looking for something they can say about the brand that could not be claimed by any other brand. The danger is that doing so achieves nothing because the unique feature is seen by most customers as having little relevance to their buying decisions—the fax machine with "smallest footprint in its class" syndrome.

As we noted earlier, it is not a coincidence that the USP concept came from an advertising man or that many advocates of differentiation based on unique brand attributes, such as Al Ries and Jack Trout, started in advertising.[10] Those advocates know from practical experience that effective advertising has to be distinctive to capture the customer's attention, or achieve cut-through, amid all the other stimuli to which people are exposed today.

The problem comes from extending this insight from advertising and other communications about the brand to the underlying offer and strategy. The brand (i.e., your named product or service and its associated price, availability, etc.) is not the same as communications (e.g., advertising) about it.[11] When your overall strategy is to provide generic category benefits simply better than the competition, your communications are unlikely to succeed by just stating that directly. Most consumers will give no credence or even attention to a paid-for claim that you deliver things they care about simply better. Your advertising will just get lost.

It is reasonable to assume that, as common sense suggests, marketing communications are usually ineffective unless the customer or prospect is aware both of the communication and of which brand it is for.[12] What is true is that merely exposing a brand's name and logo can increase its levels of familiarity and awareness, salience, perceived size, and even trustworthiness. The earlier Alliance & Leicester case focused on an awareness-raising TV campaign. The advertising worked mainly because it was noticed—no mean feat in such an information-laden society.

All animals, including humans, respond more to novel than to familiar stimuli. Even small babies give more attention to objects that are new to them or different from other things in a room or a picture. The same applies to adult customers and prospects. The implication? If you want people to notice your communications, make those communications distinctive as well as relevant. Capturing people's attention is only the beginning of the communication process, necessary but not sufficient for success. But if you fail here, you will not get any further. Creating effective marketing communications is easier said than done, so here is a simplified five-step approach that should help.

Disciplined Creativity: A Five-Step Process

One of the frustrations of people in advertising is that everyone thinks they know how to do it. In reality, creating great marketing communications is extremely difficult because you try to do two things that do not easily go together. The first is to reach specific business objectives—generate qualified leads for the salesforce, support higher prices, or whatever. The second is to find a form of communication so creative that it cuts through the clutter. To achieve both of those requires disciplined creativity.

Most great artists are extremely disciplined in their work, if not always in their private lives. Tolstoy could not have written *War and Peace* and *Anna Karenina* without great discipline. But Tolstoy was a rich landowner working toward his own objectives. In contrast, when Michelangelo painted the Sistine Chapel ceiling, he had to cope with a difficult client, Pope Julius II, as well as the enormous artistic, technical, and physical demands of the task itself. The issues in marketing communications are the same as those faced by Michelangelo—albeit hardly on the same scale. If business managers interfere too much and overcontrol the process, the work that emerges is unlikely creative enough to achieve cut-through. But without some control, you will probably end up with communications that, while possibly winning creative awards, fail to meet the business objectives.

The solution to this dilemma is not to say we need some control but not too much. It is to break the process down into semistructured stages, starting and finishing with disciplined business objectives but allowing plenty of creative freedom in between for the development and execution of communications to reach those objectives.

Probably the best and simplest formulation of this process was by Stephen King (no relation to the novelist) at J. Walter Thompson more than thirty years ago. King's framework uses the five questions shown in figure 5-2. The actual communications campaign, or execution, happens between Question 4 and Question 5.

Successful communications planning usually follows a sequence roughly similar to figure 5-2, although the questions may be implicit and the actual process is rarely as tidy as the chart implies.[13] Also, every communications agency and brand consultancy insists on using its own proprietary wording, but that changes nothing fundamental.

FIGURE 5-2

Stephen King's Five Questions

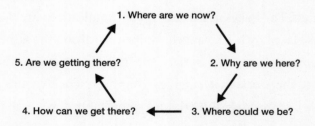

Source: Stephen King, J. Walter Thompson.

The *we* in this framework refers to the business itself and its brand equity—essentially, what customers and prospects think, feel, and do about the brand. Although the wording sounds inward-looking, it is actually customer-focused: Question 1 refers to the brand's market, Question 2 to the customer perceptions that determine or limit the brand's performance, and Question 3 to the communication objectives, again grounded in customer perceptions and actions (i.e., the intended changes in what customers and prospects think, feel, and do). Typically, the client's marketing people determine the answers to those questions based on business objectives, market research, and mainly inside-the-box thinking, although the answer to Question 2 or Question 3 may involve novel customer insights.

Question 4 asks, "How can we get there?" and is where outside-the-box thinking is essential to come up with a campaign that is sufficiently creative and distinctive to get noticed. Typically, it is the advertising or communication agency's task to develop the campaign.

Question 5—"Are we getting there?"—is another inside-the-box question involving data, hard-nosed analysis, and balanced judgment. It is again up to the client to address this question, although some agencies have econometricians and other analysts who can contribute and there are other consultancies that specialize in such analysis.

Disciplined Creativity at Land Rover

We now illustrate the process with a typical recent example—Land Rover in the United Kingdom.[14] Land Rover is a longtime off-road vehicle specialist, one of the originals that had defined the category. With the booming popularity of the 4x4 category, it found itself head-to-head with other attractive off-road vehicles. It had to get the attention of those possibly interested in the category and communicate that it was simply better at providing the category basics. This is what the company did.

Question 1: Where Are We Now?

In 2000 Ford bought Land Rover. In its U.K. home market, Land Rover was still brand leader in the 4x4 segment, which it had helped create through its own launch in 1948. Land Rover's thirty-nine thousand new car sales in 2000 gave it a 33 percent share of the United Kingdom's 4x4 category, spread across four models:

- Its original product, the no-nonsense, no-frills Defender favored by hard-core Land Rover enthusiasts and by farmers and other rural businesspeople

- The luxury Range Rover, launched in 1970

- The Discovery, launched in 1989, less luxurious and more family-orientated than the Range Rover

- The Freelander, smaller than the Discovery and aimed at a younger market, launched in 1997

Land Rover's sales were increasing slowly, but it was losing share in the fast-growing 4x4 category, which had tripled in size during the 1990s. Land Rover had once been a major player in a niche market. It was now in danger of becoming a niche player in a major market. Something had to be done. But first, it had to diagnose the situation by asking the crucial "why?" question.

Question 2: Why Are We Here?

New competitors and new customer needs had not just expanded the 4x4 category; they had also changed it. By 2000 carmakers were beginning to refer to 4x4s as sports utility vehicles (SUVs), reflecting the fact that increasingly they were bought by middle- or high-income town dwellers who liked the idea of an all-terrain vehicle but actually used it mostly for shopping and driving their kids to school. The designs of 4x4 vehicles were becoming more carlike: rounder and less angular. Some lacked the features, such as suspension, weight distribution, and low-end torque, to perform well off road, but their owners never took them anywhere rough enough to find that out.

In this changing market, consumer research showed that Land Rover still had valuable associations of authenticity, "guts," adventure, and supremacy within the 4x4 category. There were, however, signs of a recent decline in brand strength, largely attributable to a decline in perceived relevance (figure 5-3). Summarizing the problem, Wolfgang Reitzle, group VP of Ford's Premier Automotive Group, said, "Historically Land Rover has been positioned as an elephant hunter's car. The trouble is that there are only so many elephant hunters in the world."[15]

A further problem was that many consumers viewed Land Rover's four models as separate products, rather than connecting them with a coherent Land Rover brand.

Question 3: Where Could We Be?

The strategic challenge facing Land Rover was to become more accessible and relevant without compromising brand differentiation. To become more accessible, Land Rover needed to

FIGURE 5-3

Land Rover's Decline in Perceived Relevance

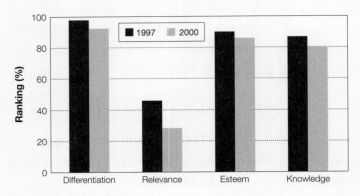

Source: Rainey Kelly Campbell Roalfe/Y&R.

become more contemporary rather than traditional; more human, spiritual, emotional, and experiential rather than remote, physical, rational, and product-centric; and more prestigious rather than functional. The specific communication objectives were as follows:

1. *Increase awareness and relevance.* Humanize and contemporize the brand—mean more to more people.

2. *Build cohesion between the models.* Develop a consistent brand identity, connect the models, and build critical mass.

3. *Add prestige to the brand.* Look at Land Rover through the lens of Range Rover, not Defender.

4. *Maintain brand differentiation.* Portray Land Rover as the current authority, not the original pioneer.

5. *Fulfill our vision of adventure.* Expand and make more inclusive Land Rover's spirit of adventure.

These five points, derived from objective data and mostly inside-the-box thinking, constituted the brief Land Rover gave to its advertising agency, Rainey Kelly Campbell Roalfe/Y&R.

Question 4: How Can We Get There?

To achieve its objectives, a communications campaign needs a single creative idea on which to hang all the specific executions. Consumer research is essential to diagnose where the brand is, why it is there, and where it should aim to be, but to find a simple idea on which to base a campaign requires creative insight, rather than just data.

In the case of Land Rover, the agency thought that the brand could become more relevant and accessible without losing its heritage and differentiation by developing the "Land Rover Experience" based on the idea that Land Rover has a positive effect on those people with an innate adventurous spirit. Communications combined two ideas: that Land Rover's owners experience more in a Land Rover because of its unrivaled product capability and that they experience more of life generally because of their adventurous spirit. The tagline in the United Kingdom was "Been anywhere interesting lately?" The tone of voice was contemporary, human, worldly, and based on intelligent wit (see figures 5-4 and 5-5).

In one commercial, a young woman has invited a young man back for a late-night drink. Her loft-style apartment is decorated with artifacts from around the world. She puts on some modern ethnic music and disappears into the kitchen. He picks up a

FIGURE 5-4

Hippo Poster for Land Rover Freelander

Source: Land Rover.

strange wooden tube, looks at it puzzled, puts it to his mouth, and blows, trying to get a noise from the instrument. Suddenly, his face freezes. We cut to a framed photo of the young woman standing in front of her Freelander with a group of tribesmen from Papua New Guinea. We see they're covering their modesty with wooden tubes exactly like the one he's trying to blow from. The woman comes back with wine and glasses. Embarrassment all around. . . .

The campaign theme and tone of voice were used consistently across a wide range of communications, including advertising in a range of media and the Internet, among other channels (figure 5-6).

Question 5: Are We Getting There?

Both the TV commercials and the posters achieved high levels of advertising awareness, likability, and brand recognition;

FIGURE 5-5

TV Commercial for Land Rover Freelander

Source: Land Rover.

that is, people noticed the ads, enjoyed them, and knew that they were for Land Rover. The perceived relevance of the brand regained some of the ground lost in the previous five years, despite competition from several new model launches by other 4x4 manufactures. This increase in relevance was achieved without compromising the brand's differentiation, which continued to score well on "best off-road," "tough," and "authentic." Most important, U.K. sales increased by 15 percent between January 2001 and December 2002. Overall, the campaign was both effective and efficient, and Land Rover has used many of the elements in the United States and other countries.

FIGURE 5-6

Land Rover's Range of Communication Channels

	Advertising	Internet	Corporate identity	CRM	Literature/ POS	Auto shows/ Exhibits	Events/ Promotions	Sponsorship	PR
Relevance and awareness	TV ●	Global Web site ●						Tomb Raider ●	
Coherence	The Land Rover Experience ●		Look and Feel Guidelines ●						
Prestige							Mario Testino Exhibit ●	Duke of Edinburgh Awards ●	Range Rover Launch ●
Differentiation				Off-Road Experience Centers ●	Off-Road Imagery ●	●			
Adventure				●			G4s Challenge Event ●		

Source: Land Rover.

The Communications Brief: Unnecessarily Constraining the Strategy

Out-of-the-box creative advertising starts with a clear inside-the-box objective about who the target market is and what you want those people to think, feel, or do in response to the campaign. This communications objective should follow from your business objective.

A Constraining Brief:
The Reading and Literacy Campaign

Sometimes, however, clients try to impose unnecessary constraints that are anything but liberating. For example, a successful U.K. government campaign to combat illiteracy among children, especially boys in low-income households, would have achieved nothing if the advertising agency had not challenged the brief.[16] The brief, although clear in its objective to encourage more parents to help their young children learn to read, assumed that the reason that working-class parents do not read with their children is because they do not appreciate the benefits of literacy. However, research among working-class parents quickly showed that they wanted the best for their children, recognized that being able to read was a necessary life skill, and accepted that they as parents had a potential role to play. That research identified the real reasons why parents were not reading with their children:

- Parents felt they didn't understand how to do it.

- They, particularly men, did not accept their personal role: they thought it was the schools' job not their own.

- They did not have time.

- They did not want another bedtime chore.

Those insights gave the agency a good understanding of the crucial diagnostic question "Why are we here?" But in order to exploit it, the creative team needed some out-of-the-box thinking. This provided a simple solution to the "How can we get there?" question: Reading did not have to be just books at bedtime; it could be anything, anytime, including reading cereal boxes at breakfast, road signs from the car, CD covers at home, and so on. Those were natural reading opportunities that occurred spontaneously in everyday life. Advertising could validate those reading moments and encourage parents to exploit them. Such opportunities were all valid, fun, and easy, and fathers could get involved.

The resulting campaign involved a leaflet distributed mainly through schools and two TV commercials alternating shots of a book at bedtime with everyday reading moments. The effect was dramatized by the use of a famous nursery rhyme interspersed with words from the everyday occasions. Both parents and teachers noticed and liked the commercials, and literacy increased significantly.

The reading and literacy example illustrates several key aspects of successful marketing communications. First, valid *customer insight* ("Why are we here?") is an essential precondition. Second, for a memorable campaign that cuts through the clutter, you need a *simple, creative, out-of-the-box idea*—the main theme of this chapter. Third, *set clear objectives, but do not unnecessarily constrain how they are met*. Finally, *use communication channels in combination*—in this case TV commercials and a leaflet.

A Liberating Brief: The Orange Launch

In contrast to that example, the launch of Orange involved ambitious objectives with wide freedom for the agency to develop a creative campaign to achieve them. The goal was to create a strong, premium brand, exploiting the incumbent cell-phone companies' strategic mistake in allowing the business to become commoditized. Orange developed the following ambitious brand vision:

There will come a time when all people will have their own personal number that goes with them wherever they are so that there are no barriers to communication. A wire-free future in which you call people, not places, and where everyone will benefit from the advances of technology.[17]

The one guideline on execution was that Orange's advertising must never feature anything remotely resembling a cell phone! The campaign was targeted at the mass consumer market and aimed to make customers think and feel that "The future's bright, the future's Orange."

The campaign was highly distinctive and extremely successful. It won numerous prizes for both creativity and effectiveness and has influenced the tone of many subsequent mobile-network campaigns around the world. Orange's success was achieved by combining the operational excellence discussed earlier with a clear vision for the brand and by allowing the ad agency wide scope for communicating that vision. The one constraint imposed—no cell phones—was enormously liberating since it focused minds away from the technology itself and toward its functional and emotional benefits to customers.

After the Campaign: Disciplined Evaluation

After the campaign, you should go back to inside-the-box thinking. Question 5 ("Are we getting there?") involves data analysis and evaluation to assess these three things:

1. How *effective* was the campaign? To what extent did it meet its objectives in Question 3?

2. How *efficient* was it? How big was the impact relative to the resources consumed? Were the benefits more than the costs?

3. What did we *learn?* Can this campaign help us do better in the future?

The most challenging part of campaign evaluation is to decide what sales and prices would have been without the campaign, as with any investment decision or postaudit review.[18] It should be possible to get a reasonable answer for most direct marketing, short-term sales promotions, and direct-response advertising where the aim is to stimulate a short-term response. For brand-building advertising, you usually need a range of metrics, including various measures of brand equity.[19]

Keeping a Sense of Perspective

It is important to keep a sense of perspective about marketing communications. *Brands* are crucial, but few are created primarily by *branding*—packaging, advertising, the brand name, and so on. As we saw earlier, branding cannot create a strongly differentiated niche brand within a category; most so-called niche brands are just small. Most great brands—Disney, IBM, Sony, and others—are based on many years of customers' experience buying and using products and services under the brand, which is supported by excellent communications. There are some exceptions, such as luxury fragrances (Dolce & Gabbana, Calvin Klein, and Chanel), where branding is central. Many mass-market brands (e.g., Coca-Cola) are based on a combination of product, distribution, and branding, with branding again playing a crucial role.

All great brands are built on a bedrock of trust derived from customers' experience of buying and using products and services sold under the brand name. The resulting brand equity is then reinforced by excellent branding, which usually plays a supporting role. Of Interbrand's ten most valuable brands in 2002, only Coca-Cola (#1) and Marlboro (#9) have been created primarily by branding that's supported by a good product and great distribution.[20] Intel (#5) owes some of its strength to its "Intel Inside" branding campaign but more to its products' price performance, its strategic alliance with Microsoft, and its dominance of standards. The rest of Interbrand's top ten—Microsoft (#2), IBM (#3), General Electric (#4), Nokia (#6), Disney (#7), McDonald's (#8) and Mercedes-Benz (#10)—are primarily customer-experience brands.

Marketing people would do well to keep that in mind. Marketing in the narrow sense—what goes into the marketing budget—usually plays a supporting role to the product or service, alongside its price and availability relative to the competition's. That is why we have waited until this chapter to focus on out-of-the-box thinking. It needs to be mainly confined to communications and should happen only when everything else is in place. In contrast, marketing in the wider sense—aligning the whole organization to meet customers' needs better than the competition—is at the core of business success. Most truly customer-focused companies are also good at marketing communications based on clear business objectives and powerful customer insights. The other element needed is great, out-of-the-box, creative ideas and execution.

IDEA CHECK

Are your communications both disciplined and creative?

1. Where is your brand? Why is it here?

The first question should be easy to answer if you have the right metrics and diagnostics. The second requires deeper customer insight and possibly soul-searching.

2. Where could you be? How can you get there?

You need to consider a range of possible objectives and strategies and then to focus on the best. For the actual communications, you need a big idea. If you do not have one, keep going—or keep your ad agency going—until you do.

3. Are you getting there?

You must measure effectiveness (Did the campaign reach its objectives?), efficiency (Was it good value for money?), and learning (What have you learned that will help you do better in the future?) in that order.

4. Are you using the full range of communication channels?

Different channels are better for different tasks. New channels are starting to come into their own. The customer must see an integrated brand across all the touch points.

Customer-Focused Mind-Set

It is an immutable law in business that words are words, explanations are explanations, promises are promises, but only performance is reality.[1]

—Harold S. Geneen,
former chairman, International
Telephone and Telegraph

Toyota—Focusing on the Basics in the Luxury Market

Toyota entered the U.S. market in 1957, a time of big gas-guzzlers, well before the first oil crisis. Initial impressions of Toyotas were of quirky, small, low-quality Asian cars. Those perceptions slowly evaporated as motorists reported satisfaction with the cars' excellent reliability and value for money. Eventually, with U.S.-based state-of-the-art manufacturing facilities, Toyota built its position as the world's most efficient manufacturer of quality cars for the masses. The Toyota advantage was shown vividly by McKinsey consultants who compared sales price, incentives, and residual values of the Toyota Corolla and the Chevrolet Prism—identical cars except for the name, designed by Toyota and manufactured on the same assembly line.[2] Although General Motors spent $750 more per car than Toyota in buyer incentives, the Toyota outsold the Prism by a factor of four and held its value longer. Perceived quality had real market value.

The late 1980s represented an important departure when Toyota developed the Lexus, its first venture into the luxury end of the market. Could it leverage mass-market quality in that market? What would *quality* mean? In the case of Lexus, it meant dealing with the basics to perfection. The key to understanding the otherwise well-known Lexus success story lies in Toyota's customer-focused mind-set.

Toyota Luxury: Pursuing the Essentials

During the early 1980s, affluent baby boomers favored foreign brands like Mercedes-Benz and BMW over domestic brands like Cadillac. Toyota saw European brands as weak on such issues as price and the cost of maintenance. Its research showed that the primary motivation for Mercedes buyers in the United States was "prestige image" based on the brand's long-established European and engineering heritage. Toyota believed that there would be a market, even among many Mercedes buyers, for a better value luxury car. The design brief suggested that Toyota realized that basic performance as a vehicle could be a primary motivation for buyers—even at the high end of the market:

A luxury sedan with a sense of intelligence which excludes gimmicks and pursues the essentials, . . . a car with a respect for human beings, which moves not automatically, not wastefully,

but faithfully by the driver's intention. . . . We are going to pro-
duce the ultimate luxury car based upon our 50 years of experi-
ence in manufacturing an automobile.[3]

In addition to redefining luxury, Toyota would also need to find
new or better ways of communicating prestige. A Toyota report
stated:

We cannot sincerely communicate such a prestige image without
having all the "facts" to satisfy customers; not only having the
best product, but also in creating the best showrooms, with the
most sophisticated sales manners and the best after-sales ser-
vice—all being customer oriented.[4]

Toyota's design and engineering team had to rethink what
luxury meant in practice. For example, team members had observed that the running cost of many luxury cars increases with
age, so they would have to find ways to eliminate the main causes
of depreciation and long-term maintenance costs, such as rust
and deteriorating paintwork. In pursuit of that aim, Toyota
bought several competing vehicles and evaluated them for dete-
rioration on ninety-six different dimensions of technical performance. Flaking chrome plating and uneven fading of interior
color, considered normal by competitors, was simply unaccept-
able to Toyota. Its design team increased the thickness of the
chrome plating by a factor of eight, adopted heat- and sunlight-
reflecting window glass, and painted the body with six coats.
When the car was left in the desert for a year along with the competition's cars, it suffered no weathering and emerged in much
better condition than the rest.

The new Lexus dealership would comprise eighty dealers selected from fifteen hundred who had initially expressed interest. Many owned Mercedes and BMW dealerships. Only those with the highest customer satisfaction index (CSI) scores were seriously considered. Applicants had to submit business plans and

- provide documentation of delivering both high CSI and sales leadership within their primary market area;

- produce a record of profitable dealer operations;

- demonstrate an understanding of the high level of personalized service expected by luxury car buyers; and

- commit to the capital ($3 million to $5 million) and staffing investments to ensure a consistent customer experience.

Toyota's commitment to make owning a Lexus an exceptional experience by extreme attention to the basics was tested fewer than three months after launch. Lexus received *one* customer complaint regarding a cruise control malfunction and several complaints about one of the brake lights. Its response was to recall all eight thousand cars sold in the first quarter prior to receiving any regulatory guidance. Dealers contacted all owners personally and made the repairs quickly. The cars were returned washed and with a free full tank of gas. Takao Kawamura, head of U.S. after-sales service, led the recall decision. He commented:

Lexus wanted to proceed in a manner that was beyond customers' expectations. We believed that the bottom line of prestige image was a feeling of trustworthiness. . . . Lexus is not a mere name of a model or a franchise; . . . it is a "culture" developed from Customer First [at an early stage in the development of the Lexus brand, divisional executives had selected being the leader (#1) in customer satisfaction as their quantitative common goal that would be shared throughout from the staff at Lexus HQ to all dealer employees. This goal, and the consensus achieved in determining it steered all behavior and decisions to a consistent end].[5]

Lexus launched in the United States with the LS 400 in January 1989. A year later, the car was voted number one in *all* categories, including customer satisfaction, in *Car and Driver*'s New Buyers' Study. It had also become the number-one luxury import, selling more than seventy thousand cars, more than either Mercedes-Benz or BMW. In 1991, Lexus ranked number one overall in J.D. Power and Associates's Customer Satisfaction Survey.[6]

Toyota's Compass: The Toyota Way

"The Toyota Way" defines the company's expectations and guides its behavior. That phrase is as close as anyone can come to describing the company's culture, and it guided the Lexus launch in the United States. In 2001 Toyota codified The Toyota Way (figure 6-1). Fujio Cho, Toyota's president, saw it as an important tool for enabling new members of the fast-growing global Toyota family to understand "the unique and outstanding elements of [the] company's culture and success."[7] Implicit throughout is that all activities enable Toyota to make great cars and provide great service—that's it.

The Toyota Way 2001 encompasses five concepts that support two main pillars: continuous improvement (including challenge, *kaizen,* and *genchi genbutsu*) and respect for people (including

FIGURE 6-1

The Toyota Way 2001

Challenge

We form a long-term vision, meeting challenges with courage and creativity to realize our dreams.

- Creating Value Through Manufacturing and Delivery of Products and Services
- Spirit of Challenge
- Long-Range Perspective
- Thorough Consideration in Decision Making

Kaizen

We improve our business operations continuously, always driving for innovation and evolution.

- *Kaizen* Mind and Innovative Thinking
- Building Lean Systems and Structure
- Promoting Organizational Learning

Genchi Genbutsu

We practice *genchi genbutsu* . . . go to the source to find the facts to make correct decisions, build consensus, and achieve goals at our best speed.

- *Genchi Genbutsu*
- Effective Consensus Building
- Commitment to Achievement

Respect

We respect others, make every effort to understand each other, take responsibility, and do our best to build mutual trust.

- Respect for Stakeholders
- Mutual Trust and Mutual Responsibility
- Sincere Communication

Teamwork

We stimulate personal and professional growth, share the opportunities of development, and maximize individual and team performance.

- Commitment to Education and Development
- Respect for the Individual; Realizing Consolidated Power As a Team

Source: Internal Toyota Documents.

respect and teamwork). In the preface to The Toyota Way, Cho set out his expectations:

We are never satisfied with where we are and always improve our business by putting forth our best ideas and efforts. We respect people, and believe the success of our business is created by individual efforts and good teamwork. All Toyota team members, at every level, are expected to use these two values in their daily work and interactions.[8]

This relentless focus on pushing, moving forward, and doing better appears to work. Toyota has enjoyed spectacular success in the United States and is well positioned to capitalize on the increasing liberalization of the EU market. Its market capitalization of $87.7 billion is higher than the combined market value of DaimlerChrysler, Ford, and General Motors.

The Toyota success story is not one of product engineering genius, although the maker of the world's first commercially produced hybrid car, the Toyota Prius, and many other product firsts, may disagree. Nor, historically, has it been one of style, no matter how proud the executives at Toyota Europe are of the Yaris, winner of the coveted European Car of the Year in 2000. Nor is it about emotion, although Toyota's entry into Formula 1 motor racing in 2002 is starting to bring more emotion to the brand. J.D. Power and Associates, however, has consistently recognized Toyota for a platform of quality performance built in at the factory as number one in the auto industry. Although the brand leaves some "gear-heads" cool, more than six million car buyers a year around the globe disagree. The basics matter and, when focusing on them, Toyota adopts a customer-first perspective and wins—even in the luxury market.

Toyota's customer focus and relentless innovation reflect a successful simply better organizational culture. In this chapter, we explore what an organization-wide customer-focused mind-set is like across a range of companies, and why it matters. This mind-set underlies all the execution best practices in the previous chapters.

From Market Information to Customer Responsiveness

Our starting point is how companies learn about markets. Earlier we discussed immersion—direct customer contact in the actual buying or usage context—as well as understanding competitors and the use of customer dissatisfaction data to identify generic category benefits with scope for improvement. We also argued that companies need formal market research to complement their impressions from direct immersion. But none of this market information achieves anything unless the company learns from it and responds appropriately. In this chapter, we argue that an organization's underlying values ultimately drive its ability to both sense and respond to market signals.

We then explore how successful companies develop a culture that is appropriately responsive to customers, using what we call "fast and right" processes since speed of response is also crucial in competitive markets. We discuss such companies' direct learning from the market, their decision-making process, and the role of accountable experimentation. Finally, we summarize the key features of the "pure air" culture underlying these fast and right processes.

How Companies Learn About Markets

In 1997, when we first investigated senior executives' opinions in the United Kingdom about customer focus, we were surprised to find that only 234 out of 434 top managers (54 percent) agreed with the statement "We measure customer satisfaction systematically and frequently."[9] That statistic suggested a less than universal commitment to customer focus. Five years later, the proportion agreeing with the same statement *dropped* to 20 percent. Several factors account for that decline. Response rates to satisfaction surveys have dropped as customers have got fed up with being surveyed. Companies also say that satisfaction scores are a poor predictor of loyalty and tell one nothing about the causes of dissatisfaction, so they are not actionable.

There is some truth in each of those gripes, but you should still measure customer satisfaction to show short-term and local changes in how well you are meeting customers' expectations and to monitor more general, long-term trends. Keep the measure as simple as possible and be prepared to offer a prize or other incentive to get an acceptable response rate, or use a syndicated source such as the American Customer Satisfaction Index. The data—like all data—has its limitations. It must be used in combination with other information and insights. Customer orientation is a commitment to meeting customer needs without overcomplicating things or running around in circles. It is based on listening but also requires formal data collection from the market. In itself, however, data achieves nothing.

How Companies Waste Market Research Expenditure

We estimate that, at the end of the 1990s, global expenditure on third-party market research had reached $18 billion annually, a threefold increase during the decade. About $2.5 billion of that was directed at measuring customer satisfaction. Unfortunately, we suspect that much of this effort reflects a bureaucratic defense mechanism. Executives are under pressure to have answers about what is going on in their markets. Given the abysmal level of customer satisfaction, we can only assume that much of the huge expenditure on market research is to help clients satisfy and impress their bosses, rather than to understand what is going on and react. Academic research in this area supports that suspicion: Many managers use research results to justify already formed positions.[10]

At a global capital-goods organization we observed, two teams of executives drawn from different product groups were given the same detailed market study and asked to interpret the results and recommend to the corporate center how the company (not necessarily their business unit) should approach the opportunity. Neither group knew that the other had been asked the same question. Each made a compelling argument that its own product was the perfect solution and explicitly showed why the other group's product was unsuitable. In isolation, each case was impressive, persuasive, and apparently customer-focused. But taken together with the other group's case, each had clearly used the data to support its own position. They used the data for support, not for illumination. This situation is fairly typical.

How Companies Actually Learn
About What Customers Value

Curious as to what was really going on, we asked senior U.K. executives about how their companies learn about customers and competitors, how much different functions interact to create customer value, and their businesses' underlying value systems.

Not surprisingly, we found a strong claimed belief in the value of achieving a good understanding of customer needs. *Customer sensing* is commonplace. The most significant statistically observed difference in the approaches to understanding customers between the high- and low-performing companies is that in the most successful ones, managers of *all* departments—finance, administration, operations, and so on—are in regular contact with customers, getting a better, more realistic understanding of the customer experience. As described earlier, there is also an important difference in how those meetings take place. In short, business meetings on current issues are most effective, and social interactions don't help so much. We also found formal *competitor sensing* to be much less widespread and to tend to be undertaken disproportionately by high-performing companies. Perhaps it is this combination that enabled 74 percent of respondents in the high-performing companies, compared to only 44 percent of respondents in the low-performing companies, to claim, "All our managers understand how everyone in our business can contribute to creating customer value."

Again, the focus is on the CEO's perception that *all* managers have that insight. Those findings suggest that high performers are not slaves to the questionnaire or the formal process but understand and act on the essence of Peter Drucker's assertion so many years ago:

> *Marketing is so basic. . . . it encompasses the entire business. It is the whole business seen from the point of view of its final result, that is, from the customer's point of view. Concern and responsibility for marketing therefore must permeate all areas of the enterprise.*[11]

And high performers are, of course, the exception. Generally, marketing does not permeate all areas of the enterprise. As Fred Webster, of the Amos Tuck School at Dartmouth College, has argued, it has tried to—and that may be part of the problem.[12] We agree with him that functional marketing needs a home: marketing communications, branding, market research, and insight building need investment and nurturing. We contend, however, that the role of marketing in achieving a companywide adoption of Drucker's idea is to be the chief drumbeater supporting top management's efforts to promote ubiquitous customer focus. Marketing can orchestrate, guide, and provide technical assistance. It can summarize, persuade, and classify. But it must not be the champion. That ground can only belong to the CEO.

Our study convinced us that, although companies were widely engaging in customer sensing activities, especially formal market research, those activities were often ineffectual because, deep down, managers were unable or unwilling to respond to customers' needs and demands. This observation led to our model of customer orientation and how in practice it works to enhance business performance (figure 6-2).

FIGURE 6-2

How Customer Orientation Really Works

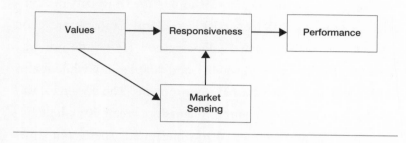

How Values Drive Both Market Sensing and Customer Responsiveness

Our data suggested that, while market sensing can be valuable, it was not the primary driver of customer orientation. Its effect on performance was indirect. Equally, if not more critical, was the degree to which the organization was responsive to what it learned about the market. The organization's value system—what really mattered, its culture—drove both the nature (but not the extent) of market sensing and the degree of responsiveness.

Getting an objective measure of a complex construct such as organizational culture or values, including where the customer fits in, is difficult. Asking managers whether customers are important is, in any form, folly. Rather than crudely asking respondents to describe their culture in terms of the customer's role or priority, assessing it indirectly through the competing values approach can tell us more about actual customer focus.[13] Our research suggests that companies that (1) value openness and flexibility and (2) are more concerned with external rather than internal matters are more likely to be customer responsive and enjoy superior performance.

George Day of the Wharton School of the University of Pennsylvania suggests that General Electric and Citibank are good examples of such so-called adhocracies.[14] He points out that these companies value "flexibility and adaptability while maintaining a focus on the external environment." The dominant values of an adhocracy are entrepreneurship, creativity, adaptability, autonomy, and willingness to experiment. These companies value growth, acquisition of new resources, and innovativeness. They are diametrically opposite to the bureaucratic archetype, the hierarchy.

Hierarchies tend to be inward-looking and rigid, prioritizing order and routine. Although one might expect them to perform well in mature industries and stable markets, our data suggest that, irrespective of the industry (high tech/low tech, products/services, B2B/B2C) the more bureaucratic an organization is, the less likely it is to be commercially successful. However, a company with no bureaucracy at all would suffer from insufficient direction and control. Adhocracy needs to be deliberate, and the behavior it tolerates needs to align with companywide objectives. Perhaps surprisingly hierarchy can play an important role.

How Hierarchy Can Improve Performance: Swiss Re America

A clear sense of hierarchy can deliver efficiency and effectiveness and can actually *reduce* unhelpful bureaucracy according to Jacques Dubois, chairman of Swiss Re Life and Health America Inc.[15]

Cost consciousness is an obsession for Dubois, who tells his executives that "service is the refuge of the inefficient." That philosophy does not reflect an anticustomer approach—quite the contrary. Dubois demands that his executives focus on precisely what delivers customer value. His point is that the service offered should be in line both with the company's strategy and with customers' interest and willingness to pay. Too often it is neither. Dubois attributes his cost consciousness to the stringent terms imposed by the backers of the leveraged buyout of the General Reassurance Company he led in 1988. Small negative variances would have derailed the entire deal. His approach was to keep everything focused and simple.

Dubois agrees that it is critical for the top of an organization to be intimately familiar with what is really going on in the market. He observes that managers often see themselves as delegators, which he believes is dysfunctional since delegating puts decisions in the hands of potentially inadequately qualified people. Dubois goes further: "By raising decision making to the highest level possible, we get to see our people in action. It motivates them. They deal with the top." There were few standing committees, but meetings happen as needed. Decisions get made.

Lorenzo Zambrano, CEO of giant cement producer Cemex, uses information systems to cultivate an entrepreneurial and energetic organization.[16] His systems place him in direct contact with all elements of the massive company. He can monitor plant productivity globally and in real time. If he detects that a plant's operating levels are below the benchmark for the other forty-nine plants, he can call a worker directly to find out why. If he wants to check out how sales worldwide were in the past twenty-four hours, he can. That capability has changed how Cemex people manage their time and work. They no longer have to stop what they are doing to look for information. The data is readily available.

As with Swiss Re and Cemex, both of whom find virtue in sensible hierarchy to enhance customer responsiveness, the high-performing companies we observed tended to be flexible and claimed to have the ability to respond and adapt to changing market conditions. Also, employees felt that they were treated well and were a part of the "deal." Respondents suggested that in terms of those values that provide a shared sense of purpose in their companies, sometimes referred to as "organizational glue," these high-performing companies value loyalty and tradition as well as innovation, and development over mindless microman-agement characterized by an overemphasis on goals, tasks, rules, and policies. Creating a flexible organization that is responsive, focused, and efficient thus involved managing a duality.

How Companies Manage the Duality

We attribute companies' ability to manage the duality—flexi-bility plus order and efficiency—to their transparency and inclu-siveness. One CEO told us that the two most critical drivers of employee morale were (1) understanding the company's strategy (i.e., being able to make sense of what it was doing from day to day) and (2) having faith in the ability of your immediate boss to contribute effectively to making the strategy a success. That combination is more than just pleasant. It has a decisive impact on how the organization treats information and, therefore, the rate at which it learns about and responds to events in the mar-ket. In high-performing companies, trust is high and market in-sights are relatively depoliticized.

So, being customer-focused is not about corporate rhetoric, nor is it even just about market sensing. It is about the ability to create continuous learning regarding the market and to respond appropriately to what is learned. This responsiveness appears to be dependent on, or at least interdependent with, the underlying organizational culture. Creating a culture that is appropriately responsive is thus imperative for those seeking to be simply better.

Creating a Culture That Is Appropriately Responsive to Customers

Customer responsiveness is intuitively appealing: Develop your organization's ability to understand what customers want and need, know what else is or could be offered, and let nothing stop you from providing the right solution. This is clearly simplistic, however; organizational rigidities exist for a reason, usually to do with achieving operating efficiencies and economies of scale that allow you to operate at a cost level that is attractive to most customers and competitively sustainable. We hope it is clear that we are not suggesting that being responsive to customers means that you always give them whatever they want—being what George Day calls "customer-compelled," like IBM in the early 1990s.[17] So what is customer responsiveness, and why does it matter?

What Customer Responsiveness Is and Why It Matters

Customer responsiveness means being fast and right in the eyes of customers.[18] To explore this view, together with Charlie Dawson of The Foundation, a London-based consultancy specializing in this area, we interviewed ten high-profile U.K. CEOs with marketing backgrounds, including Peter Davis, CEO of Sainsbury; Luc Vandevelde, chairman of Marks & Spencer; Peter

Burt, chairman of Bank of Scotland; and Eric Nicoli, chairman of EMI Group. Collectively the interviewees appeared to see customer responsiveness as "accurately and insightfully giving customers what they need, want, or don't yet know they want. And . . . consistently doing so more quickly than anyone else and rapidly enough to retain the value of the decision or idea for customer."[19]

The value of being right about customer needs is obvious. But the value to both the customer and the business also depends on the speed of the response. Satisfying customers is usually not that hard; it simply takes time and money to get things right. With enough testing and piloting most companies get there in the end. Being fast is not that hard, either. Being both fast and right, however, presents a challenge.

A fast and right culture is not a risk-taking, "failure is good" culture. Interviewees conveyed both intolerance of doing the wrong thing and impatience about responding too slowly. Practically speaking, to enhance customer responsiveness, companies should embrace three key sets of behaviors that lead to both faster and better decisions. We call these direct learning, hardwork decision making, and accountable experimentation. These behaviors are supported by what we call a "pure air" culture (figure 6-3).

Why Impatience and Intolerance Enhance Customer Responsiveness

The particular form of learning, decision making, and resource allocation represented in figure 6-3 is based on the politically incorrect notion that impatience and intolerance are good.

FIGURE 6-3

Fast and Right Processes and a Pure Air Culture

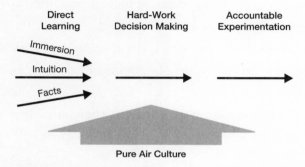

Pure Air Culture

Source: Seán Meehan and Charlie Dawson, "Customer Responsiveness: Getting It Fast and Right Through Impatience and Intolerance," *Business Strategy Review* 13, no. 4 (2002): 32.

Direct learning increases a team's ability to make the right decisions using judgments based on immersion, intuition, and fact-based market research. We discussed the effectiveness of immersion earlier. Many executives interviewed characterized the intuition of managers who were immersed in real market experiences as a crucial competitive tool. Intuition is especially important in creative industries, such as television, fashion, and music, where every episode, design, or song is a new product and formal market research is a poor predictor of market response and can discourage risk taking. Eric Nicoli, chairman of the EMI Group, a record and music-publishing company, pointed out that the reinvention of a pop singer like Robbie Williams or the discovery of bands like Coldplay and Radiohead happened because individuals had instinctively sensed these opportunities and fought hard for them. To the executives interviewed, fact-based market research then provides a basis for checking the validity of at least some opinions about market opportunities, backed up by the judgment derived from immersion and intuition. Also, some market research, such as pretesting advertisements, can help improve execution.

Hard-work decision making is about replacing frantic activity with rigorous debate within a better informed team, using high standards to avoid wasting effort. One place where hard-work decision making is essential for success is Silicon Valley.

Fast and Right in Silicon Valley

Stanford professor Kathleen Eisenhardt and her coresearchers compared the behavior of top management teams in highly successful and less successful Silicon Valley companies.[20] The key difference was in the quality of those companies' debates.

The best management teams expressed their disagreements frankly without generating interpersonal conflict. They did that by focusing on current factual data, building multiple alternatives, creating common goals, developing a balanced power structure within the group, and using humor to release interpersonal tensions. In contrast, the less successful teams relied on opinions, wishes, and guesses; focused on only one or two alternatives; ignored common goals; let autocrats or, at the other extreme, laissez-faire rule; and had less fun.

Another difference was in the behavior of the leader. Willingness and the ability to listen are essential attributes of all good managers, but such listening is not a sign of weakness—on the contrary. In the successful management teams, if discussion of an issue did not lead to consensus, the leader decided, guided by input from the rest of the group. It is crucial that even those who had argued for a different course of action usually threw themselves wholeheartedly into executing the decision once it was made—if they believed the leader genuinely listened to their views. This approach, sometimes called "consensus with qualification," limits conflict and leads to fast and right decisions, at least in comparison to decision making by fiat or deadline, or endless debate in a fruitless search for consensus.

Early Turnaround Versus Long-Term Success

Ideally, a successful organization would have many empowered individuals all capable of making fast and right decisions. It is hard to get to that stage. The key seems to be clear, top-down guidance of thought and action, but not detailed prescription, as the dominant way of working. The mitigating factor is that it be based on up-to-date objective facts and on what is right for the customer. Depending on the stage that the company is at (early turnaround versus long-term success), this top-down approach works in different ways.

In a turnaround situation, when *fast* often matters more than *right,* an experienced, small, and coherent team can provide effective direction. But the decision-making group has to expand to sustain success over the long term. This happens as others in the organization interact with the top team. Rather than acting as a bottleneck, such interaction serves to educate this wider group about the degree of market intimacy that must underpin all key initiatives. Intolerance for ideas that are not firmly rooted in the reality of the marketplace is seen as a positive force for change, "purifying" the organization's thought process.

Purification takes time but eventually ensures that everyone involved in debating issues and making decisions has a shared basis for interpreting market dynamics. Until this shared view is in place, the small top team must make the big decisions. Over time, by being involved in these debates and decisions, more and more people around the business understand the high standards and the unyielding process. Those who are going to be able to live with it, and thrive on its exacting consequences, will stay and enjoy more autonomy as a reward for understanding the approach.

Tesco illustrates what the process is like once a business is well established on a successful path. At Tesco, a clear and well-understood vision for the business made it possible to push responsibility a long way down: Buyers had one meeting every six months where they set out their plans to hit their numbers. They had the ability to dictate launches, promotions, and pricing. The onus was on the individual buyer to make it work: There was clear overall direction and lots of freedom for initiative, but if something did not work, it was clear who was responsible. This approach was popular with suppliers (packaged-goods manufacturers) and focused on customers: Suppliers found Tesco less bureaucratic and more responsive than its competitors.

Accountable experimentation requires a combination of widespread good-quality learning and high hurdles for decision making to ensure that, when trials do happen, they are already building on considerable data, thought, and discussion. This method has the benefit that a smaller group of well-informed bright people can operate better and faster than a disparate group running multiple uncoordinated trials. Also, by having fewer experiments, each gets more attention and is carefully set up and planned.[21]

Companies committed to accountable experimentation still expect mistakes. Indeed, in our research on customer responsiveness executives expressed the view that if there were no mistakes then the organization had not been trying hard enough.

Some interviewees talked about seven out of ten as the kind of hit rate they were looking for—high and exacting but not risk-free. This tolerance of 30 percent failure was also expressed as an acceptance, enthusiasm even, for U-turns and valuing people's ability to spot an unsuccessful experiment while they were working on it and to close it down. As we saw earlier, one of Progressive Insurance's strengths has been its ability both to experiment and to be ruthless in stopping any experiment that imperils its outstanding business system. Similarly, Hilti's exploration of new market opportunities includes accountable experiments, such as its cautious move into retail distribution.

"Pure Air" Culture

Underlying direct learning, hard-work decision making, and accountable experimentation in the successful organizations we studied was a "pure air" culture. The pure air culture was not comfortable or cozy. Rigor and unyielding standards appeared to be important elements of the way these companies operated.

The first feature of a pure air culture is that challenge and debate are seen as forces for good, not just by the top management team but throughout the organization. Because the process of discussing conflicting ideas and views is based on facts and objective observation, it encourages people to share learning and build judgment.

The second feature is that no one expects an easy yes to proposals. By requiring people to make a strong case to get the go-ahead, the organization toughens up but also fully values opportunities when they do arise. Peter Burt, chairman of Bank of Scotland, spoke enthusiastically about an executive who had championed a problematic mortgage plan for elderly homeowners. The executive had been rebuffed several times but did not give up.

Consequently, this pure air system purges poor argument and lack of rigor. While a balance must always be struck between fast and right, compromise is avoided where possible. There are not fewer ideas being discussed and progressed, just fewer bad ones. Like purer air, this is a clearer environment within which strong people and strong thinking can thrive.

David Robey, Tesco's former director of corporate marketing, described the company in the mid-1980s and early 1990s as being like the Wild West. It was aggressive, highly disciplined, and very can-do but fair with no hidden agendas. People were allowed to challenge and take chances. If they succeeded, even if they were difficult characters, they were highly valued. Conversely, if they failed too often, they were out.

Creating such a fast and right approach to customer responsiveness is difficult. It requires clear leadership and signaling. For a start, top management needs to show its commitment through direct learning. Consider the case of Berkeley Homes described earlier. After his visit to the building site, chairman Tony Pidgley appeared to be moving toward a fast and right approach. He certainly wanted customer-focused action. His week on-site represented one part of direct learning, and, critically, it resulted in his moving the company toward a pure air culture. Think of the impact on his management team when, at a meeting, he produced the irrefutable physical evidence of substandard work. When one manager asserted that, despite Pidgley's evident disappointment, they had the will to do right by the customer, Pidgley exploded: "We haven't got a will here . . . I'm not having it today that we've got a will. We talk about it, I write memos. . . .

None of it is in place. . . . It's lip service."[22] Pidgley's week on the building site totally reenergized him. His direct learning had made him the authority on customer service.

Just as thinking outside the box was the expected approach for managers in the 1990s, we expect a return to fundamentals to become today's big idea. Back to basics is already gaining ground as the new staple of the executive suite. We can expect headlines like "GE Chairman Goes Back to Basics" to become widespread.[23] We do caution, however, that a successful return to basics is not about slashing and burning parts of your business; rather, it is about being simply better. This requires far more than doing more market research. It is a commitment from the top to transform the entire culture of the business—starting at the top itself.

Companies that embrace true customer focus start with a crystal clear view of what their business is about and how they create customer value. Unlike competitors that tend to be whimsical and sometimes distracted by the latest big opportunity, the companies we have highlighted, while engaging in many often complementary activities, do not have an identity crisis. Toyota designs and builds great cars. Hilti is second to none in the world of high performance professional drilling and demolition technology. Tesco is a grocery retailing star. All the leaders of these companies share a passion for the customer, and they and their management teams demonstrate that through action—the resulting stories of important customer interactions become the stuff of corporate legend. Direct, frank customer interactions matter to individual managers who are empowered to do something to respond. Those interactions are the primary source of meaningful customer insight. All our examples are obsessed with delivery and execution—because in the end that is what the customer gets. Ryanair is all about execution around a simple proposition—low price. Orange, Procter & Gamble, and Progressive Insurance all built massive shareholder value through focusing on execution. And because they are thinking of what really matters to customers, they clearly execute their strategies with category needs in mind, rather than slicing and dicing markets and developing unique strategies around those needs.

IDEA CHECK

Are you serious about customer responsiveness?

1. Does your organization have clear values and beliefs?

Written or not, yes it does. The question is, is everyone's interpretation consistent? If you believe in customer focus, help everyone understand what that really means—what behaviors should be expected in which circumstances.

2. Are business cases well supported with current, factual market data?

Market research reports are often abused. Ensure that case promoters have a good understanding based on both firsthand experience and hard data.

3. Do you tolerate a lot of trial and error?

Don't. Limit the resources available for such trials, but do attach some sort of cost to them. Trials without costs or consequences for the advocate lead to sloppy thinking.

7

How to Be Simply Better

Only the paranoid survive.[1]

—Andrew Grove,
chairman and CEO of Intel

Procter & Gamble—Back to Growth

By any standards, Procter & Gamble (P&G) is a star. By the late 1990s, it was one of the best known, most successful, and most admired companies in the world. It had been feted as visionary in *Built to Last,* James Collins and Jerry Porras's influential study of companies that have consistently delivered extraordinary returns to shareholders over the long term.[2] Collins and Porras found that homegrown talent was one of the factors that distinguish visionary companies from their peers. P&G was known for its homegrown talent.

Durk Jager was appointed CEO of P&G in January 1999, only the tenth CEO since the company was incorporated in 1890. Having joined P&G in 1970 straight out of college, Jager fit the

Built to Last model. His experience of the organization was impressive. Until rising to vice president in 1987, he had held a series of increasingly senior positions in brand management and regional operating management. In 1990 he was promoted to executive vice president with responsibility for the soap, chemicals, health, and beauty divisions in the United States and in 1991 became head of the company's whole U.S. business. In 1995 Durk Jager was appointed president and chief operating officer and in 1999 CEO. But his reign as CEO was the shortest in P&G's history—a mere eighteen months.

As CEO, Jager took the path of a revolutionary. His watchwords were *innovation, stretch,* and *change.* Perhaps this was to be expected given his predecessors' record. In each of the five decades from 1940 to 1990, P&G had achieved the increasingly difficult goal of doubling sales. Jager's attempts to increase the dynamism of the $40 billion company, however, did not have the desired effect. Quite the opposite—it was a disaster. In the six months prior to his departure, P&G lost 50 percent of its market value, a staggering $70 billion (see figure 7-1).

Organization 2005

In September 1998, Jager was still COO. Concerned that there was insufficient further room for P&G's flagship brands, such as Tide, Crest, Pampers, and Folgers, to drive continuing growth, he embarked on an ambitious plan—Organization 2005—to enhance dramatically the company's ability to bring major new products to market fast.[3] P&G would invest heavily to create and nurture these billion-dollar brands of the future.

This strategy was a radical change for the company, which had recently become better known as a grand master of selling incremental product improvements than for radical breakthroughs.

FIGURE 7-1

P&G Ten-Year Share Price History (January 1993 to August 2003)

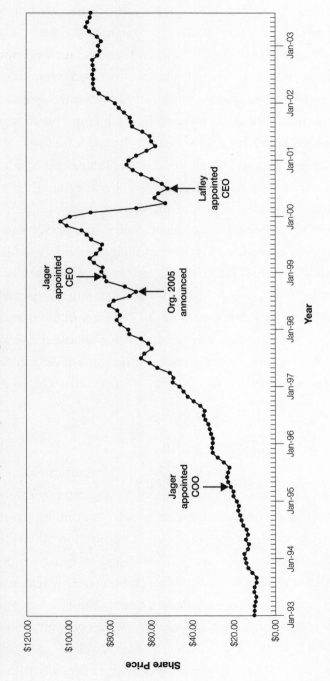

Source: http://finance.yahoo.com

The new strategy would require management to rethink everything from structure to work processes and culture. It would eliminate fifteen thousand jobs and ten plants. P&G would be reorganized into seven global businesses based on product lines, with reduced authority for local country management. The restructuring would cost a one-off $2.1 billion, and savings were projected at $600 million annually.

To make Organization 2005 work, Jager believed his managers needed to be more focused and energized. They needed to change what he saw as a somewhat unchallenging approach. Jager praised organizations like General Electric that had delivered strong results and attributed their success to management attitude.[4] He said that General Electric had been ambitious and repeatedly changed the rules of the game in its favor. He castigated what he characterized as the P&G self-fulfilling prophecy of a cautious "promise low" culture that could never lead to good performance. "You have to create a revolution," he said, calling on managers to

- reconceive product concepts,

- redraw market boundaries,

- reshape the industry structure,

- reframe the challenge, and

- reject the status quo.

Jager's approach involved launching new products, transferring support from old established brands like Tide and Pampers to new hopefuls, which, if successful, would power P&G's future growth.

Europe was one of P&G's toughest environments. Culturally diverse, it had a highly concentrated retail structure within each country that put pressure on both volumes and margins. With the aim of increasing growth while cutting costs, Jager encouraged the different country organizations to adopt identical, Pan-European brand positions, packages, and even names. Thus Ariel in Europe and Dash in Italy, big detergent brands that stood for different things, were to be standardized not only within Europe but also with U.S. Tide. In Germany, a new fabric softener variant was called Downy, rather than the well-established Lenor brand. Subsequently, when the very well-known Fairy dishwashing liquid adopted its American name, Dawn, market share plummeted.[5]

In search of a much-needed breakthrough, P&G's laundry detergent marketers dug deeper than ever before to try and uncover consumers' real motivations. The result? The European mass-market laundry detergent Ariel came out in a new guise: Ariel Essential. Responding to Jager's call to think outside the box, managers had completely reformulated the product's value proposition. Ariel would now offer more than just excellent cleaning; it would also promise the benefit of actually enhancing the clothes. The brand would now be positioned more like a vitamin, with healing and protection properties, rather than in its previous well-established position as a highly effective stain remover. Again market share plummeted. Such moves, together with trying to force a new way of doing business on retailers, led the overall fabric-care business downhill.

Nor was this just a European phenomenon. When P&G pushed ahead with a new pricing strategy in the United States, it suffered adverse trade response. The CEO of Stop and Shop said

P&G was "acting like a dictator" and warned, "We will do everything in our power to undermine their plans." Supervalu added a special surcharge to P&G lines, while some other wholesalers discontinued them.[6]

Back to Basics

After Durk Jager's departure, P&G abandoned the new way and out-of-the-box thinking and returned to the basics. It immediately began to reverse the market share decline it had experienced in Europe over the previous five years. Chris Warmoth, head of P&G's fabric-care business in Western Europe at the time, commented:

> *Frankly, our issue on [Western Europe] fabric care over the past five years has not been lack of vision or choices—but rather the wrong vision and choices. . . . [The choices we made] simply weren't rooted in consumer or [trade] customer reality. If successful, they would have indeed changed the rules of the game—but we discovered the particular consumer and customer rules weren't for changing. We discovered that we weren't after all the boss.*[7]

Over the previous century P&G had been an exemplary inside-the-box player with a well-earned reputation for successful product innovation. Its approach had been evolutionary, not revolutionary. With its ambitious Organization 2005 program, the company temporarily lost sight of the basics. It got distracted. It tried to run too fast and stumbled. Now, post-Jager, it has regained its strengths. Jager's successor is A. G. Lafley, who was appointed in June 2000 and got his start twenty years earlier as a brand assistant for Joy dishwashing liquid. Lafley, the so-called un-CEO, has adopted a low-key, back-to-basics approach:

Even when you've got a complex business, there's a core, and the core is what generates most of the cash, most of the profits. The trick was to find the few things that were really going to sell, and sell as many of them as you could.[8]

P&G's stock dropped a further $4 on news of Lafley's appointment. Since then, however, it has made back much of the previously lost ground. By the end of July 2003, it had climbed to $89, bucking the downward trend in the overall stock market.

The point of this story is not that any old company can lose its way. Many do. Nor is it that, with determination, any old company can recover from a diversion. Many cannot. We are not describing just any old company. We are talking about Procter & Gamble, an outstanding company with $40 billion in revenues and more than a hundred thousand employees in eighty countries. This is the company that brings you well-known brands such as Pringles, Pampers, Cover Girl, Bounty, and others. The point is that, however good you are, simply better is hard work requiring continuous attention.

Many companies struggle, like P&G, to stay energized and to achieve and sustain growth. It is easy to become distracted. We offer six straightforward rules that will help you stay the course to become, or perhaps stay, simply better.

Rule 1: Think Category Benefits, Not Unique Brand Benefits

In the late 1980s, a student at London Business School summarized the whole of what he had learned during the first year of the M.B.A. with the words "the Japanese do it better." What we argue in this book has much in common with total quality management (TQM) and *kaizen,* or continuous improvement. Today, the Japanese economy is in a rut, and its exporters have difficulty competing overseas, but the best Japanese companies such as Toyota, Honda, Sony, and Canon are still world leaders, especially in product innovation, manufacturing techniques, and quality control. Their continued success is all the more remarkable given the difficult conditions under which they operate: a depressed domestic market, ferocious competition (especially from other Asian companies), the low dollar, and the fact that others in those industries have now had more than a quarter-century to copy their approach.

Perhaps it is time to look again at the books on Japanese management that have been gathering dust on your shelf since 1988. However, *Simply Better* goes further than those books in two respects. First, whereas Japanese management mainly focused on the manufacturing function, we argue that the approach should be applied to *every function in every industry*. In particular, we think there are often opportunities to improve service quality—and every business is at least partly a service business in the minds of its immediate customers.

Second, TQM and especially *kaizen* tend to take an internal, engineering-driven focus. As applied by a company such as Toyota, the benefits are there for all to see. As consumers, we should all be grateful for the resulting improvements in price performance and reliability we now take for granted in so many products. In this book, however, we argue that this internal process focus needs to be complemented by an external focus on customer needs and especially on those needs that are already identified but not well met or, as in Orange's case, those needs that are obvious but are not even being addressed. Hence, we focus on customer dissatisfaction data, both to counter complacency and to suggest specific opportunities for improvement.

Most companies today collect regular data on customer satisfaction and/or perceptions at the brand level. But most industries are so set in their ways that they have trained customers to accept something like the existing levels of product and service quality and the attributes on which brands compete. Sometimes it takes some digging and imagination to unearth important needs that have not been articulated and are not being well met. Note: These are *category* needs. To unearth them, you need to ask customers, and sometimes noncustomers, about what they like and especially what they dislike about the *category*. This feedback will guide you toward the differentiation that matters.

Compelling examples abound: Orange's creation of £13 billion more shareholder value than One2One. The Daewoo U.K. launch. Shell's discovery that many customers would switch to a gas station with a clean bathroom. Virgin Atlantic's launch on the premise that, since consumers find long-haul flights boring, they will appreciate decent movies and an ice cream before landing. So Rule 1 is to focus on what customers like—and especially dislike—about the category, not just about your brand and your competitors' brands.

Rule 2: Think Simplicity, Not Sophistication

Shell sees itself as a company that aims to meet the energy needs of society in ways that are economically, socially, and environmentally viable, now and in the long term. Most of us, however, think of Shell as a supplier of fuel and lubricants at our local gas station and as an oil and gas explorer and producer. We know that Shell is huge and global. We are less aware of its gas- and power-marketing business, its chemicals business, or its emerging hydrogen, solar, geothermal, and wind energy businesses. Partly reflecting Shell's visibility in the introduction of new important management techniques—notably scenario planning—many managers rightly regard the company as progressive and sophisticated.[9] Many know that it recruits really smart people who work with good resources on exciting projects. By the nature of its business, Shell seems long term and strategic. You may, however, be quite surprised to learn that Shell is also one of the world's largest single-branded retailers. Its global network serves some *25 million customers a day* in more than fifty-six thousand service stations.[10]

Pat O'Driscoll was certainly surprised to learn those statistics. The well-kept secret of Shell's retailing scale did, however, explain why a headhunter working on behalf of the company's global retailing business was calling her. O'Driscoll's retailing credentials could hardly have been better. She had spent her managerial career at Tesco, Safeway, and Marks & Spencer, a leading U.K. retailer. O'Driscoll was sufficiently intrigued with the challenge described by Shell that she joined it in 1997. After an initial eighteen months working with the team developing the global retail strategy, she was assigned to oversee the $30 billion European retail operation—and its fourteen thousand gas stations—to implement some of the proposals and methods that she and the team had developed.

What struck O'Driscoll about Shell was that, in contrast to the retailers she had worked for before, it had little sense of who its retail customers were and what they really wanted. Shell was a global powerhouse, highly successful over many years and full of clever people, but its executives did not have a retailing mind-set. O'Driscoll felt that they believed that she, with her strong retail background, was about to come up with a silver bullet. Who could blame them? After all, a recent *Wall Street Journal* article headline read "Mobil Bets Drivers Pick Cappuccino over Low Prices."[11] The article described how sophisticated segmentation analysis had identified at least five different types of gasoline buyers in the United States: Road Warriors, True Blues, Generation F3 (those who want fuel and food, fast), Homebodies, and Price Shoppers. Each segment had its own distinct needs and, by catering to them, Mobil had significantly enhanced its performance. The initiative, dubbed "Friendly Serve," had apparently raised revenue by as much as 25 percent in some participating stations. Clever stuff.

The outcome of O'Driscoll's work, however, took Shell in a direction different from catering to the distinct needs of a variety of customer segments. She concluded that, although it would be possible to find distinct segments and treat them differently, gasoline retailing is a fundamentally functional category. Drivers overwhelmingly want to refuel at a reasonable cost; be sheltered from sun, wind, and rain while they do so; and pay and exit quickly. They expect the pumps and bathrooms to be clean and working. With Shell, motorists have an expectation of choice and innovation in the refueling offer. They are not looking, first and foremost, for a great cappuccino.

Understanding its customers' priorities and ensuring that they were consistently satisfied on the basic attributes enabled Shell to become their preferred refueling option. The initial performance improvement of 20 percent increase in like-for-like sales in Shell's major European markets settled down at about

10 percent. Return on capital, which had been zero prior to the initiative, soon reached double digits and exceeded targets.

The initiative was challenging because the company had to introduce so many frontline employees to the new approach. The change involved many difficult steps, including closing almost half of the existing outlets and coping with the inevitable short-term dip in employee morale. Employee skepticism changed, however, when the initiative started producing results. Transparency, simplicity, and consistency were key. For example, in the past, regional managers were hammered on costs, yet many stations were supposed to be open 24/7, despite seeing virtually no customers for six to eight hours. Local managers were empowered to do what made sense, as long as they excelled on the basics. Morale shot up. Engaging senior management was also crucial: It needed to appreciate what was really going on. Site visits, including holding business review meetings in the field, became the norm. Data giving the daily, weekly, and monthly performance updates helped speed decision making to respond to customer and competitor challenges.

Sophisticated? Hardly. Effective? Undoubtedly. Nevertheless, resisting the teenage urge in all of us to look clever can be difficult when surrounded by smart, enthusiastic colleagues. That is why we think that it is important, as a rule, to think simplicity, not sophistication.

Rule 3: Think Inside, Not Outside, the Box

The alarm bell went off when, a few years ago, a senior executive (let's call him "Jim") at a major consumer-goods company congratulated one of us on our counterintuitive thinking. Having spent the day explaining how customer value orientation works to enhance business performance, we were surprised by his reaction.

Jim's business, it turned out, was the cash cow of his organization. In his five years in charge, he had consistently delivered on-target earnings. His market share was high and stable, and customer satisfaction ratings were so high that other business unit heads had ceased to benchmark against him. Colleagues, however, suggested that the business's success was attributable not to Jim's management but rather to the colossal brand he had inherited. They would regularly ask, "What has Jim done with the business? Where are his innovations? Doesn't he realize that if he continues with the old model, the competition will overtake him?"

Jim believed that managers had increasingly become thrill-seekers who had lost sight of the fundamental economics of risk. The late 1990s bull market had issued not so much a license to be brave but an edict. Executives from all disciplines multitasked, coordinated, visioned, and strategized. Simply taking care of the business had somehow become passé. With no meaningful acceptance of the downside inherent in risk, Jim argued, the trend-conscious executive was doing lots of novel stuff: Between exploring Web opportunities, sizing up the next acquisition candidate, restructuring the balance sheet, partnering, venturing, and outsourcing what they once thought was their core activity, managers had taken their eyes off the ball. They had been encouraged to do so and were often rewarded irrespective of outcome. They were having a ball. They were excited. They were learning lots in their exploration of the new futures they would fashion. Who could blame them? They had, after all, been endlessly encouraged to think creatively, out of the box. They had repeatedly been urged to break the rules.

All this made Jim feel like a dinosaur. What excited him was creating value for his customers, one at a time. Although the revenues of Jim's division exceeded $2 billion, he knew all his major customers (large retailers), their businesses, and their issues. His knowledge of consumer trends and his ability to understand how and why they evolved as they did were legendary. He was intimately involved in product development and, with his team, had created an operations and fulfillment capability that was the envy of the industry. He was, simply, a profit-and-loss man, a complete business manager. He knew how to build and nourish a mature business, getting everyone enthused about creating customer value. "Simple blocking and tackling" is how he put it to us. What is counterintuitive about that?

We urge you to think twice before breaking too many rules. Just as most clichés are clichés because they are usually true, rules are there for a reason and generally make some sense. Instead, redirect your creativity. Look at how your customers really make buying decisions and what matters most to them. Be realistic and frank when discussing worthy competitors. Confront disappointment with confidence that you can and will improve. Do not get distracted from monitoring the performance of your businesses and all your competitors' businesses on the generic category benefits.

It was Jim who told us that if he hears "think outside the box" one more time, he'll scream. We agree with him. Is it not about time managers spent more effort thinking about the basics of their business, more effort thinking about real customers? Is it not about time they saw that we—the customers—are easy to please? We simply expect companies to deliver on their promises. Too many managers have spent so much time outside the box now that they have forgotten how good it can really be when they strive to be simply better.

Rule 4: Think Opportunities, Not Threats

Business success is elusive. When you find it, you should enjoy it. Yet companies seem to fall into the quite different traps of inaction due to complacency, and of paralysis due to excessive caution.

Complacency born of security makes no sense at all. Demographic evolution changes your customer base over time. Technological innovations open up new possibilities. Consumer preferences evolve. Moreover, as we've discussed, categories themselves evolve. Of course, existing and new competitors are out to steal your lunch. All these forces, and more, will impact every business.

Evolving your offer, innovating to drive the market, is difficult because it is so hard to mobilize employees. Further, when you've figured out how to be simply better, you need to protect the fundamentals of your business system against would-be rule breakers. With all this in play, paranoia should be the order of the day. Be complacent about market shifts and you will suffer, just as Kirin Brewery did. In 1987, when the much smaller Asahi Breweries, with a 12.5 percent market share, launched its now world-famous Super Dry beer, Kirin's market share was 57 percent, based on its 90 percent share of all *lager* beers sold in Japan.[12] In just under ten years, Asahi's flagship outsold Kirin Lager by 6 market share points to become the number-one beer brand in Japan with 33 percent of the total market.

Kirin's mistake was to ignore the changing demographic profile of Japan. Younger drinkers were becoming more important, and their tastes and lifestyles were different from those of the older drinkers who accounted for Kirin Lager's success. Demographics do not change overnight. They change one life at a time—steadily and predictably.

Inaction due to insecurity can be even worse than inaction due to complacency. When, over the years, customer response confirms that you have found a great way to execute and that your offer is valued highly, there is an understandable fear of rocking the boat. Opportunities to evolve, by, for example, adopting a new technology, come along. The pressure not to adopt stems from the fear that doing so will probably cannibalize your existing business. We suggest that what distinguishes those companies that take the risk and adopt the new technology is that they have a superior understanding of what customers really want. Take Gillette.

Gillette first created (in 1903) and then dominated the mass market for disposable safety razor blades. In 1962 its position appeared unassailable with a remarkable 72 percent market share.[13] Yet, within just one year, it had lost almost a third of this to the small British company Wilkinson Sword, whose new stainless-steel blade lasted three times longer than Gillette's carbon-steel blade.

Gillette had been aware of the new stainless-steel technology for some time and had even licensed some of it to Wilkinson Sword. But Gillette had been reluctant to adopt the new technology. Why? Because doing so would have rendered obsolete much of Gillette's manufacturing capacity for carbon-steel blades. Wilkinson might have taken over the whole market if it had had enough capital. But ultimately, as researchers Gerard Tellis and Peter Golder note, "The Wilkinson experience galvanized Gillette to innovate even at the cost of cannibalizing its own established products." Tellis and Golder are referring to Gillette's Trac II twin-heads razor (1972), Atra pivoting-head razor (1977), GoodNews twin-blade razor (1978)—a response to a serious threat by Bic disposable razors—and, Sensor, a razor with twin blades that move independently (1989).

Now, years after the Wilkinson threat, innovation is "almost an obsession" at Gillette. Gillette's perspective on what it takes to win is rather telling. The key, it says, is to "provide benefits people think are worth paying for"—generic category benefits such as a quicker, closer, more comfortable shave. Gillette brands are supported by a technology stream fueled by a corporatewide understanding of the customers' most basic category requirements and, therefore, of what R&D should focus on.

Whether potential changes are caused by new technology, government intervention, a changing customer base, or whatever, think of them as opportunities, not threats.

Rule 5: For Creative Advertising, Forget Rule 3

If your essential proposition is to meet basic category needs better than the competition, you may have a problem making yourself heard. The solution is to adopt a distinctive, out-of-the-box approach to persuading skeptical customers that you have addressed their core needs and created a business system to provide those needs better than your competitors. Inside-the-box advertisements and other communications do not work. This is where you or the creative people at your ad agency really do need to think outside the box.

Daewoo did this with great effect. As part of its strategy, it needed to persuade U.K. motorists that, because Daewoo sold direct rather than through dealers, they would experience a hassle-free buying process, peace of mind, and courteous after-sales service. When Daewoo tested its concept, it felt the full force of market cynicism. Car buyers had heard it all before. One interviewee said that car manufacturers are "all mouth and no trousers."[14] In addition, Daewoo had to make itself heard in a very heavily advertised market. With a combined market share of 51 percent, the three largest manufacturers each spent anything from £25 million to £50 million annually advertising on network TV, in the national press, and on billboards. Daewoo's launch budget was £10 million. Like Alliance & Leicester, it used humor throughout its campaign along with reinforcing its simple message: We're on your side. Indicative of its approach is the competition it ran offering viewers a chance to become one of two hundred "guinea pigs"—drivers who would be given a free Daewoo for an extended yearlong test drive (see figure 7-2).

The ad opens with a close-up of a man telling the viewer about Daewoo's offer. On his mentioning guinea pigs, two hundred of the little creatures appear. He gives up, leaving the voice-over to restate the message and invite the viewer to participate. The offer, together with its advertising execution, captured the market's attention. Two hundred thousand people called the toll-free number to be a guinea pig, totally swamping Daewoo's phone lines.

Studies by Millward Brown, the leading authority in tracking advertising effectiveness, supports Daewoo's belief that this and

FIGURE 7-2

Daewoo's Out-of-the-Box Advertising Achieved Almost Universal Awareness

Voice-over: After fifteen years of making cars all over the world, Daewoo are coming to Britain. And as part of the process, they're looking for guinea pigs to test drive two hundred Daewoo cars for a year, free. [Enter two hundred guinea pigs.] . . . Come on, you know what I meant.

Voice-over: If you'd like to be one of the two hundred test drivers, call and tell us why we should pick you. Daewoo, the biggest car company you never heard of, would like to hear from you.

Source: Daewoo's Advertising Agency, Duckworth Finn Grubb Waters.

other advertisements in the campaign helped it overcome its awareness problem and position itself effectively as a customer-focused car company. Supplementary research showed that, remarkably for a car company, Daewoo had achieved a position of trust. Consider these comments from consumers:[15]

> The impression I have is that they're more honest than the others.
>
> They're a good company . . . straight, with their cards on the table.
>
> They won't rip you off.
>
> They're not too glossy. I like that. They cut out all the bullshit.

Millward Brown's quantitative tracking studies showed Daewoo's brand awareness to be near universal, its approach seen as both unique and customer-focused. Against huge odds, Daewoo sold a lot of cars in its first year. Part of that success was based on highly creative outside-the-box advertising and publicity.

Out-of-the-box brand communications similarly aided Orange, another simply better company. One of Orange's golden rules was never to feature a cell phone or anyone using one in its advertising. Orange's people-centric brand positioning is all about simplicity and straightforwardness. Its execution was so unlike anything in the category that with this combination of simplicity, straightforwardness, and transparent and fair pricing, Orange made impressive inroads in the public consciousness. Tracking studies showed that Orange enjoyed greater awareness than either of the big incumbents, Cellnet and Vodafone. Other studies identified smart advertising as a key contributor to Orange's shareholder value creation.

Rule 6: Think Immersion, Not Submersion

Several of the companies described in *Simply Better* demonstrate that immersing yourself in the realities of your marketplace is not just a way to find and prioritize opportunities. It is also key to energizing your organization and keeping it focused on what really matters. Our advice? Insist that the whole company, not just the top management and the sales and marketing people, gets regularly immersed in the market. The more you do that, the more successful you will be in creating a customer-focused mind-set. There is no substitute for direct market access from the top to the bottom of your organization.

Unilever learned how critical getting the whole company involved was when it was ambushed by P&G in 1994. P&G proudly ran advertisements displaying boxer shorts it said had been ripped to shreds by Persil Power, the latest version of Unilever's top U.K. detergent brand. Unilever had introduced the new product after careful development and testing. "We believed there was nothing wrong with the detergent," said Niall Fitzgerald, then head of Unilever's $10-billion-a-year detergent business. The market thought differently. P&G's claim stuck, and at an estimated cost of hundreds of millions of dollars, not to mention 5 percent market share, Unilever withdrew Persil Power.[16] During one post-mortem meeting, Fitzgerald asked the thirty-one senior executives assembled whether any of them had actually washed their own clothes in the past six months—not one had. They were out of touch.[17]

Is it unusual for senior executives to be out of touch? No. Simple economics argues in favor of specialization. But distance and specialization carry hidden costs, reinforced by the fact that people tell the boss what they think he or she wants to hear, so problems get buried rather than discussed and addressed. Shareholders may sympathize with the idea that top management should focus on the "grown-up" tasks: corporate strategy, resource allocation, investor relations, corporate communications, and running the overall business. Managers today work long, long hours at a relentless pace. It is hard not to drown in the workload. But senior managers are well paid and get plenty of support at work and at home, so they do not have to spend time on the mundanities of day-to-day living such as doing the laundry. Do executive VPs at any car company actually shop around for their own cars? Do senior bankers have to go through what the rest of us have to in order to get a mortgage?

In the name of efficiency, senior executives generally outsource most of what they regard as distractions to support staff at work and at home. But some of these distractions are, in fact, the stuff of opportunity. They are sources of the unpleasant and unreasonable frustrations consumers experience every day: the broadband connection that gets discontinued by mistake, the franchised car dealer that keeps you waiting half an hour to get your car back after servicing, the beautifully packaged toy that breaks into pieces when the birthday child unwraps it.

Unilever, like many other leading companies, has instituted customer-contact programs that aim to push understanding of customer and consumer reality right through the organization. Hindustan Lever, Unilever's 51-percent-owned Indian subsidiary, is exemplary in this regard. It requires new recruits to spend six weeks living with a poor family in a remote Indian village. Niall Fitzgerald, now cochairman of Unilever, argues that this practice ensures, at every level, that the organization knows the reality of consumers' lives.[18] Apparently arguing for the enrichment of market research to compensate for its tendency to dehumanize people (e.g., reducing them to abstract "segments"), he believes this initiative ensures that "from the very beginning [recruits] understand who our consumers are, . . . [and they are not] some great amorphous aggregate. They are individuals who live in 150 different countries." In other words, the six-week field experience of Hindustan Lever's new recruits enables them to see everything from the consumer perspective in order to bring the voice of the consumer to the table during any key decision. The more people who share the customers' perspective, the better.

When you are through with this paragraph, put the book down. Go to your calendar. How many whole days in the next four weeks are dedicated to interacting with buyers (those who make decisions to acquire your product or service) and with users or consumers (those who use it)? Get the point? Now clear your schedule. In the next month, make it a priority to visit customers on their own turf—big and small, near and far, new and old, and especially dissatisfied and lapsed customers. Focus on observing and talking to customers *where and when they buy and use your brands and your competitors' brands.* As you struggle to find space in your calendar, remember Rule 6. It is immersion in the customer experience, not submersion in your other workload that matters. Although administration, resource allocation, and high-level strategy are important, take them in moderation. Bite the bullet. You may be surprised by the impact.

A One-Minute Summary of the Argument

Companies are not as customer-focused as they think. Everyday experience and customer surveys bear that out. At the root of the problem are two assumptions, both wrong. First, companies assume that they need to offer something unique to attract business. Secondly, they assume that years of competition have turned the underlying product or service into a commodity. In reality, what customers care most about is that companies reliably deliver the generic category benefits, but, far too often, that does not happen. Therefore, most businesses have a big opportunity to beat the competition, not by doing anything radical and certainly not by obsessing about trivial unique features or benefits, but instead by getting closer to their customers, understanding what matters most to them, and providing it simply better than the competition.

And Finally

Being a customer, whether at home or at work, accounts for a high proportion of our waking hours. Often it is a bad experience. This represents a huge opportunity for companies serious about putting customers first. In *Simply Better* we have spelled out what we think putting customers first means in practice. A reviewer of a recent book on excellence in customer service cited several examples from his own recent experience where the featured companies, including some very good companies, had "bad hair days."[19] The pièce de résistance was where the reviewer tells how he settled down to read the book as his Eurostar train pulled out—late—of Brussels station. His original train had been cancelled with no apology or explanation. (This was soon after Eurostar left passengers stranded for five hours outside London's Waterloo Station). Imagine his reaction on finding the managing director of Eurostar quoted three times in the book on his company's wonderful customer-led culture. Did that director have any idea of customers' actual experience with the brand?

There is often a wide gap between the intent and the experience. Companies have to reconnect. One way to start the process may be to turn the discussion at the next informal outing with colleagues to disasters they have experienced personally as customers of other businesses—we all have them. Now work through one or two of those experiences in more detail. How on earth could they have happened? Could it happen at your company? Of course it could—worse, it already has. But now, with an acceptance that unforced errors will happen, tackle what you can do to improve. As Michael Dell observes: "Everything can be done better. There is nothing that cannot be improved."[20]

In putting the customer center stage we urge managers to reassess how well they really understand what customers want. Every company serious about customer focus should aim to be the best at the things that matter to customers.

This is a never-ending story for two reasons. First, you never get the basics right. If you did, you would presumably achieve a 100 percent customer satisfaction score, and even then you would likely lose it as soon as you took your eye off the ball. Second, there are always opportunities that will require you to increase the complexity of your business or look to new opportunities. But, as the Tesco.com example discussed earlier suggests, the new market opportunities where you can make money at an acceptable risk most likely build on your existing capabilities. The stronger those capabilities, the more other profitable opportunities you will have. Competitive advantage can come only from a solid foundation of knowing your customers and how they choose and delivering consistently whatever it is that matters most to them. The rest should be seen for what it is—a lottery. So start now, and never stop.

Notes

Preface

1. Michael Moncur and Laura Moncur, "The Quotations Page," <http://www.quotationspage.com/search.php3?Search=&Author=twain&C=net&x=40&y=13> (accessed on 16 January 2004).

Acknowledgments

1. Michael Moncur and Laura Moncur, "The Quotations Page," <http://www.quotationspage.com/quotes/Samuel_Johnson/21> (accessed on 16 January 2004).

Chapter 1

1. Philip Kotler, *Marketing Management,* 11th ed. (Upper Saddle River, NJ: Pearson Education International, 2003).

2. Research by telcommunications consulting firm CIT showed a projected subscriber growth rate for 1992–1995 of 75%. The actual rate, according to CIT, was 73.9%.

3. Which? Online, "Mobile Phone," December 1996, <http://sub.which.net/producttesting/reports/dec1996wh8t14/frontpage.jsp> (accessed 24 February 2003).

4. Leif Sjoblom and Xavier Gilbert, "The UK Mobile Communications Market (A)," Case GM 779 (Lausanne, Switzerland: IMD, 1998). Reference to press release by J.D. Power and Associates on 28 April 1998.

5. Ibid.

6. Which? Online, "Mobile Phone."

7. See <http://www.orange.com/English/aboutorange/philosophyandvalue.asp> (accessed 28 January 2004).

8. By *customer,* we mean the person whose category purchases and brand choices determine the company's revenue. This may be the direct customer,

especially in B2B markets, or the final consumer, as in packaged-goods markets. In the latter case, the manufacturer also has to meet the needs of retailers, or "trade customers." In all cases, the user may differ from the buyer.

9. The clarity offered by Peter Drucker, (in *The Practice of Management* [New York: Harper & Row, 1954]) did not receive much scholarly attention or empirical investigation until it was embraced by the Marketing Science Institute (MSI) as a research priority in 1988 (see Marketing Science Institute, *Research Program 1988–1990* [Cambridge, MA: Marketing Science Institute, 1988]). Subsequent investigations supported or encouraged by this MSI prioritization took two broad approaches. One approach views market orientation as a set of behaviors (e.g., Bernard Jaworski and Ajay K. Kohli, "Market Orientation: Antecedents and Consequences," *Journal of Marketing* 57 [1996]: 53–70; John Narver and Stanley Slater, "The Effect of Market Orientation on Business Profitability," *Journal of Marketing* 54 [1990]: 20–35.). The other approach sees market orientation as more of a culture or value system (e.g., Rohit Deshpandé, John U. Farley, and Fredrick. E. Webster Jr., "Corporate Culture, Customer Orientation and Innovativeness in Japanese Firms: A Quadrad Analysis," *Journal of Marketing* 57 [1993]: 23–37). Irrespective of the research approach adopted, the findings were consistent (see Don Lehmann, "Market Orientation: State of the Area," in *Research Program Monograph* [Cambridge, MA: Marketing Science Institute, October, 1994]).

10. The ACSI is a composite index, not a simple percentage. Interpretation issues are discussed by Claes Fornell et al. in "The American Customer Satisfaction Index: Nature, Purpose, and Findings," *Journal of Marketing* 60 (1996): 7–18. We take the view, however, that all customers go into a transaction expecting, or at least hoping for, total satisfaction—whatever that means for them. ACSI levels in the mid-1990s suggest that, for many customers, firms fall short.

11. Frederick F. Reichheld and Thomas A. Teal, *The Loyalty Effect: The Hidden Force Behind Growth, Profits, and Lasting Value* (Boston: Harvard Business School Press, 2001).

12. Internal Toyota Document.

13. Willie Sutton never actually said, "Because that's where the money is." But he was indeed an accomplished bank robber and jail breaker. What he really said was "Because I enjoyed it. I loved it. I was more alive when I was inside a bank, robbing it, than at any other time in my life. I enjoyed everything about it so much that one or two weeks later I'd be out looking for the next job. But to me the money was the chips, that's all." (Steve Cocheo, "The Bank Robber, The Quote, and the Final Irony," *ABA Banking Journal Online,* <http://www.banking.com/aba> (accessed 22 February 2003).

14. See Hermann Simon, *Hidden Champions: Lessons from 500 of the World's Best Unknown Companies* (Boston: Harvard Business School Press,

1996). Much of Simon's research is on world-class midsize private companies in Germany (the "Mittelstand"), but he has observed similar companies in the United States, Britain, and elsewhere.

15. Patrick Barwise, "Real Consumers, Real Purchases," working paper 2002-102, London Business School's Centre for Marketing, London, 2002. We use verbatim quotes from subjects interviewed for this project throughout this book.

16. However, contrary to what is sometimes claimed, most are not. See Peter N. Golder, "Historical Method in Marketing Research with New Evidence on Long-Term Market Share Stability," *Journal of Marketing Research* 27 (2000): 156–172. Nevertheless, a well-managed brand can have an indefinite life. See discussion of the longevity of brands in Patrick Barwise et al., "Brands As 'Separable Assets,'" *Business Strategy Review* 1, no. 2 (1990): 46–48.

17. The better mousetrap is attributed to an 1869 lecture by Ralph Waldo Emerson and discussed as a blunder in William Shanklin's *Six Timeless Marketing Blunders* (Lexington, MA: Lexington Books, 1969), 7.

18. Gerard J. Tellis and Peter N. Golder, "First to Market, First to Fail? Real Causes of Enduring Market Leadership," *MIT Sloan Management Review* 37, no. 2 (1996): 65.

19. Morgan Witzel, personal communication with author, 4 April 2002

20. James Collins and Jerry Porras, *Built to Last* (New York: Random House, 1997).

Chapter 2

1. Peter Drucker, *The Practice of Management* (New York: Harper & Row, 1954).

2. This section on Allied & Leicester is drawn from Chris Baker, ed., *Advertising Works 7* (Henley-on-Thames, Oxfordshire: NTC Publications, 1993), 359–382.

3. We are grateful to Mike Dennehy of Citibank for this telling point.

4. There are various metrics of brand familiarity or awareness. One of the most widely used is "unprompted awareness," which is the percentage of interviewees that mention the brand in response to the question "Which brands of (category X [e.g., bank, cola, car etc.]) can you think of?" In contrast, "prompted awareness" is the percentage of interviewees that mention the brand in response to the question "Which of the following brands of (category X) have you heard of?"

5. Most practitioners believe that well-liked ads tend to be more effective. We agree, although the academic evidence is mixed. See Robert East, *The Effect of Advertising and Display: Assessing the Evidence* (Boston: Kluwer, 2003), 63–64.

6. Andrew Ehrenberg, Neil Barnard, and John Scriven, "Differentiation or Salience," *Journal of Advertising Research* (November–December 1997), 7–14.

7. This explanation is a simplification. It can also be argued that the causality goes from usage to beliefs. See Daryl J. Bem, *Beliefs, Attitudes, and Human Affairs* (Belmont, CA: Brooks/Cole, 1970); Patrick Barwise and Andrew Ehrenberg, "Consumer Beliefs and Brand Usage," *Journal of the Market Research Society* 27, no. 2, (1985): 81–93; and Robert East, *Consumer Behavior: Advances and Applications in Marketing,* 2nd ed. (Hemel Hempstead, Herts, U.K.: Prentice Hall, 1997).

8. If a product that delivers the category benefits also looks different— yellow Purdue chickens or the pink *Financial Times*—it will be easier to promote. But a unique appearance will have little, perhaps no, value if competing products deliver a better combination of category benefits to most customers.

9. Kevin J. Clancy and Jack Trout, "Brand Confusion," *Harvard Business Review* (March 2002): 3.

10. Alexander L. Biel, "Strong Brand, High Spend: Tracking Relationships Between the Marketing Mix and Brand Values," *Admap* (November 1990); Andrew Ehrenberg, Kathy Hammond, and Gerald Goodhardt, "The After-Effects of Price-Related Consumer Promotions," *Journal of Advertising Research* (July–August 1994): 11–21; Carl F. Mela, Sunil Gupta, and Donald R. Lehmann, "The Long-Term Impact of Promotion and Advertising on Consumer Choice," *Journal of Marketing Research* 34 (1997): 248–261.

11. William N. McPhee, *Formal Theories of Mass Behavior* (New York: Free Press, 1963).

12. Andrew Ehrenberg, Gerald Goodhardt, and Patrick Barwise, "Double Jeopardy Revisited," *Journal of Marketing* 54 (1990): 82–91; and Andrew Ehrenberg and Gerald Goodhardt, "Double Jeopardy Revisited, Again" (R&D initiative paper, South Bank University, London, 2002).

13. Alfred North Whitehead, *An Introduction to Mathematics* (New York: Holt, 1911).

14. Eric Lapersonne, Gilles Laurent, and Jean-Jacques Le Goff, "Consideration Sets of Size One: An Empirical Investigation of Automobile Purchases," *International Journal of Research in Marketing* 12 (1995): 55–66.

15. The situation in packaged goods is often complicated by the effects of short-term price promotions. These lead to large week-on-week fluctuations in market share but have no discernible aftereffects for established brands. See Andrew Ehrenberg, Kathy Hammond, and Gerald Goodhardt, "The After-Effects of Price-Related Consumer Promotions," *Journal of Advertising Research* (July–August 1994): 11–21.

16. Strictly speaking, the metric is the *dollar-weighted* percent distribution, where each outlet is weighted by its sales of the category: Big stores matter much more than small stores.

17. Bart J. Bronnenberg, "Multi-Market Competition In Packaged Goods: Sustaining Large Local Market Advantages with Little Product Differentia-

tion," working paper 382, Anderson School at UCLA, Los Angeles, April 2003.

18. Wayne D. Hoyer and Steven P. Brown, "Effects of Brand Awareness on Choice for a Common, Repeat-Purchase Product," *Journal of Consumer Research* 17 (1990): 141–148.

19. John H. Roberts and James M. Lattin, "Consideration: Review of Research and Prospects for Future Insights," *Journal of Marketing Research* 34 (1997): 406–410.

20. Ehrenberg, Barnard, and Scriven, "Differentiation or Salience."

21. Robert B. Zajonc, "Attitudinal Effects of Mere Exposure," *Journal of Personality and Social Psychology,* monograph supplement, 9, no. 2, part 2 (June 1968): 1–27.

22. Robert Winship Woodruff, president of Coca-Cola, 1923–1985, quoted in Markus Christen, "New Coke (A)," Case 599-012-1, (Fontainebleau, France: INSEAD, 1998), 2.

Chapter 3

1. Although the version cited here is popular, Pasteur's words in fact were "In the field of observation, chance favors only the prepared mind." See Michael Moncur and Laura Moncur, "The Quotations Page," <http://www.quotationspage.com/quotes/Louis_Pasteur/> (accessed on 16 January 2004).

2. This section is based on Seán Meehan and Pius Baschera, "Lessons from Hilti: How Customer and Employee Contact Improves Strategy Implementation," *Business Strategy Review* 13, no. 2 (2002): 31–39.

3. Hilti Annual Report 2002.

4. Ewald Hoelker, interview by author, Lausanne, Switzerland, 4 February 2000.

5. John Le Carré, *The Honorable Schoolboy* (Boston: G.K. Hall, 1977), 84.

6. Four hundred thirty-four companies (31% of the sample frame), representing operating units of companies listed on the London Stock Exchange, responded to a survey of business practices. The chief executive or a designee provided answers to those mailed questionnaires. Results reported in Seán Meehan, "Market Orientation: Values, Behaviors and Performance" (Ph.D. diss., University of London, 1997).

7. Don Lehmann, "Don Lehmann Becomes Executive Director," *MSI Review* (Fall 1993): 3.

8. Bill George, interview by author, Lausanne, Switzerland, 20 September 2002.

9. Seán Meehan and Charlie Dawson, "Customer Responsiveness: Getting It Fast and Right Through Impatience and Intolerance," *Business Strategy Review* 13, no. 4 (2002): 26.

10. The week Pidgley spent on-site was recorded by a BBC film crew as part of its award winning series "Back to the Floor," screened in the fall of 1997, which documented the experiences of CEOs when they left the executive suite for a week and dealt with customers incognito.

11. Eric von Hippel, Stefan Thomke, and Mary Sonnack, "Creating Breakthroughs at 3M," *Harvard Business Review* (September–October 1999).

12. Bernard J. Jaworski and Ajay K. Kohli, "Market Orientation: Antecedents and Consequences," *Journal of Marketing* 57 (1996): 68.

13. Gerard J. Tellis and Peter N. Golder, "First to Market, First to Fail? Real Causes of Enduring Market Leadership" *MIT Sloan Management Review* 37, no. 2 (1996): 65.

14. Katarina Paddack, Rebecca Chung, and Donald A. Marchand, "The Rise of Cemex: Global Growth Through Superior Information Capabilities and Creative E-Business Strategies," Case GM 953 (Lausanne, Switzerland: IMD, 2001).

15. Richard Hunter, Ronen Melnik, and Leonardo Senni, "What Power Customers Want," *McKinsey Quarterly,* no. 3 (2003): 17–19.

16. Seán Meehan and Debra Riley, "Daewoo Motor Company U.K. (B)," Case M 528 (Lausanne, Switzerland: IMD, 1998).

17. Ben Bold, "What Must Daewoo Do to Avoid a Rebranding?" *Marketing* (16 October 2003): 13.

18. Constantinos C. Markides, *All the Right Moves: A Guide to Crafting Breakthrough Strategy* (Boston: Harvard Business School Press, 2000); and Gary Hamel and C. K. Prahalad, *Competing for the Future* (Boston: Harvard Business School Press, 1994).

19. Tellis and Golder, "First to Market, First to Fail?"

20. Stephen P. Schnaars, *Managing Imitation Strategies: How Later Entrants Seize Markets from Pioneers* (New York: Free Press, 1994).

Chapter 4

1. Chuck Frey, "Innovation Tools," <http://www.innovationtools.com/ Quotes/QuotesDetail.asp?CatID=4> (accessed 16 January 2004).

2. David Bell, "Tesco PLC," Case 9-503-036 (Boston: Harvard Business School, 2002).

3. ACNielsen, *Homescan Survey* (New York: ACNielsen, November 1998).

4. Tim Mason, "The Best Shopping Trip? How Tesco Keeps the Customer Satisfied," *Journal of the Market Research Society* (January 1998): 4–5.

5. David McCarthy, *Bankers Trust Alex Brown Analyst Report on Tesco PLC* (London: BT Alex Brown Research, April 1999): 6.

6. Sara Carter and Justin Scarborough, *Merrill Lynch Analyst Report,* 2 July 1996.

7. Mason, "The Best Shopping Trip?"

8. Claes Fornell, "The Source of Satisfaction," *Harvard Business Review* (March 2001).

9. James L. Heskett et al., "Putting the Service-Profit Chain to Work," *Harvard Business Review* (March–April 1994).

10. Bell, "Tesco PLC."

11. Lucie Carrington, "The Listener," *Human Resources Magazine* (June 2003): 27–29.

12. Seán Meehan and Pius Baschera, "Lessons from Hilti: How Customer and Employee Contact Improves Strategy Implementation," *Business Strategy Review* 13, no. 2 (2002): 31–39.

13. Ibid.

14. Bill George, interview by author, Lausanne, Switzerland, 20 September 2002.

15. Georg Tacke and Michael Schleusener, "Bargain Airline Pricing: How Should the Majors Respond?" (travel and tourism white paper of Simon-Kucher & Partners, August 2002).

16. David Neeleman, "The JetBlue Story," <http://www.jetblue.com/learnmore> (accessed on 27 July 2003).

17. See <http://www.jetblue.com/jb/difference> (accessed on 27 July 2003).

18. Simon Calder, "It's the World's Worst Airline. And I Love It," *Independent,* 25 August 2002.

19. Tom Chesshyre, "It's Cheap but Why Not More Cheerful," *Times,* 5 January 2002.

20. Graham Bowley, "How Low Can You Go?" *Financial Times,* 21 June 2003.

21. David A. Garvin, *Learning in Action: A Guide to Putting the Learning Organization to Work* (Boston: Harvard Business School Press, 2000), 139–183.

22. Joshua Mendes, "The Prince of Smart Pricing," *Fortune,* 23 March 1992.

23. Progressive Annual Report 1997.

24. This quotation and the following are from Frances X. Frei and Hanna Rodruguez-Farrar, "Innovation at Progressive (A): Pay-As-You-Go Insurance," Case 9-602-175 (Boston: Harvard Business School, 2002).

25. Greg MacSweeney, "Risks of Being on Bleeding Edge," *Insurance and Technology Online,* 8 January 2002, <http://www.insurancetech.com/show Article.jhtml?articleID=14705657> (accessed 15 January 2004).

26. Most of the examples in this section are drawn from Angela Andal-Ancion, Phillip A. Cartwright, and George S. Yip, "The Digital Transformation of Traditional Businesses," *MIT Sloan Management Review* 44, no. 4 (2003):

34–41; and Andrew J. Rohm and Fareena Sultan, "The Evolving Role of the Internet in Marketing Strategy," working paper, Northeastern University Marketing Group, Boston, 2003.

27. Patrick Barwise, Kathy Hammond, and Anita Elberse, "Marketing and the Internet," in *Handbook of Marketing,* ed. Barton A. Weitz and Robin Wensley (London: Sage, 2002), 529–557. See also <http://www.marketingandthe internet.com>.

28. Albrecht Enders, "The Tesco.com Experience: Is Success at Hand?" Case 302-083-1 (Fontainebleau, France: INSEAD, 2002), 6.

29. Ibid.

30. James Hall, "Tesco Online Delivers the Goods," *Wall Street Journal Europe,* 15–17 February 2002.

Chapter 5

1. Denis Higgins, *The Art of Writing Advertising: Conversations with Masters of the Craft* (Lincolnwood, IL: NTC Business Books, 1990), 26.

2. Constance L. Hays, "Can Target Thrive in Wal-Mart's Cross Hairs?" *New York Times,* 9 June 2002.

3. "Business: On Target," *Economist,* 5 May 2001.

4. This figure is from a presentation by Doug Scovanner, EVP and CFO of Target, to Lehman Brothers Sixth Annual Retail Seminar (reviewed by Robert S. Drbul, of Lehman Brothers in "Target Corporation: Review of Retail Seminar Presentation," 7 May 2003) in which among other topics he described what consumers liked and disliked about Target relative to Wal-Mart. It is based on a 2002 survey of Target and Wal-Mart shoppers. All differences above 0.2 percent are statistically significant.

5. Alice Z. Cuneo, "Francis's Mission: Shore Up Target's Sales by 'Owning Red,'" *Advertising Age,* 24 February 2003.

6. Robert Berner, "Image Ads Catch the Imagination of Dayton's Hudson's Target Unit," *Wall Street Journal,* 3 October 1997.

7. Alice Z. Cuneo, "Marketer of the Year: On Target," *Advertising Age,* 11 December 2000.

8. Patrick Barwise and Alan Styler, "Marketing Expenditure Trends 2003," an analysis of actual and planned marketing expenditure in the top five global markets conducted and published by London Business School, December 2003. See <http://www.london.edu/marketing/met>.

9. Rosser Reeves, *Reality in Advertising* (New York: Alfred Knopf, 1960).

10. See Al Ries and Jack Trout, *Positioning: The Battle for Your Mind* (New York: McGraw-Hill, 1981); and Jack Trout, with Steve Rivkin, *Differentiate or Die: Survival in Our Era of Killer Competition* (New York: Wiley, 2000).

11. This is the everyday use of *brand,* as in "Which brand did you buy?" *Brand* is also used in at least two other categorically different senses. First,

brand (as a noun or verb) can mean "trademark." Second, it is often shorthand for brand equity, as in "Will this strengthen our brand?" or "How does this fit our brand?" So-called brand valuation is an attempt to attribute part of the company's market value to brand equity. See Patrick Barwise, preface to *Brands and Branding,* eds. Rita Clifton and John Simmons (London: *The Economist* in association with Profile Books, 2003), xii–xv. On brand valuation, see Jan Lindemann "Brand Valuation" in *Brands and Branding,* eds. Rita Clifton and John Simmons (London: *The Economist* in association with Profile Books, 2003), 27–45; and Patrick Barwise et al., *Accounting for Brands* (London: Institute of Chartered Accountants in England and Wales, 1989).

12. Like most statements about marketing communications, this is an oversimplification and an overgeneralization. See Robert East, *The Effect of Advertising and Display: Assessing the Evidence* (Boston: Kluwer, 2003), 55–62; and Demetrios Vakratsas and Tim Ambler, "How Advertising Works: What Do We Really Know?" *Journal of Marketing* 63, (1999): 26–43.

13. This chart is inspired by Stephen King's well known five-step approach to the creative process he pioneered at advertising agency J. Walter Thompson.

14. This section is based on a presentation by Anthony Bradbury (Land Rover) and John Howkins (Rainey Kelly Campbell Roalfe/Y&R), London Business School, 7 May 2003.

15. Ibid.

16. Tim Broadbent, ed., *Advertising Works 11* (Henley-on Thames, Oxon: World Advertising Research Council, 2001), 35–66.

17. Gary Duckworth, ed., *Advertising Works 9* (Henley-on Thames, Oxon: World Advertising Research Council, 1997), 3–28.

18. Patrick Barwise, Paul Marsh, and Robin Wensley, "Must Finance and Strategy Clash?" *Harvard Business Review* (September–October 1989): 85–90.

19. Tim Ambler, *Marketing and the Bottom Line: The Marketing Metrics to Pump Up Cash Flow,* 2nd ed. (London: FT Prentice Hall, 2003), chapter 9. East, *The Effect of Advertising and Display.*

20. Gerry Khermouch, "The Best Global Brands: *BusinessWeek* and INTERBRAND Tell You What They Are Worth," *BusinessWeek,* 5 August 2002: 92–99.

Chapter 6

1. James B. Simpson, comp., *Simpson's Contemporary Quotations* (Boston: Houghton Mifflin, 1988).

2. Anjan Chatterjett et al., "Revving Up Auto Branding," *McKinsey Quarterly,* no. 1 (2002): 134.

3. Internal Toyota documents.

4. Ibid.

5. Ibid.

6. Since 1990, Toyota and Lexus have received 310 J.D. Power and Associates quality and satisfaction awards for various automobile models and manufacturing plants. Toyota and Lexus, respectively, received 129 and 42 J.D. Power and Associates awards for initial quality. Lexus alone has received 101 highest rankings for quality and customer satisfaction.

7. Fujio Cho, letter of introduction to *The Toyota Way 2001* (Toyota City, Japan: The Toyota Institute, Toyota Motor Corporation, 2001), 1.

8. Cho, *The Toyota Way 2001*, 3.

9. Four hundred thirty-four companies (31% of the sample frame), representing operating units of companies listed on the London Stock Exchange, responded to a survey of business practices. The chief executive or a designee provided answers to those mailed questionnaires.

10. Christine Moorman, Gerald Zaltman, and Rohit Deshpandé, "Relationships Between Providers and Users of Market Research: The Dynamics of Trust Within and Between Organizations," *Journal of Marketing Research*, 29 (1992): 314–329.

11. Peter Drucker, *The Practice of Management* (New York: Harper & Row, 1954).

12. Fredrick E. Webster, "Marketing Management in Changing Times," *Marketing Management* (January–February 2002): 18–23.

13. For the competing values' framework, see Robert E. Quinn and James Rohrbaugh, "A Spatial Model of Effectiveness Criteria: Toward a Competing Values Approach to Organizational Analysis," *Management Science* 29 (1983): 363–377; and Robert E. Quinn, *Beyond Rational Management* (San Francisco: Jossey-Bass, 1988). This operationalization of culture as values has been adopted in the market orientation literature. See Rohit Deshpandé, John U. Farley, and Fredrick E. Webster Jr., "Corporate Culture, Customer Orientation and Innovativeness in Japanese Firms: A Quadrad Analysis," *Journal of Marketing* 57 (1993): 23–37; and Christine Moorman, "Organizational Market Information Processes: Cultural Antecedents and New Product Outcomes," *Journal of Marketing Research* 32 (1995): 318–335.

14. George Day, *The Market Driven-Organization: Understanding, Attracting, and Keeping Valuable Customers* (New York: Free Press, 1999), 54–55.

15. Jacques Dubois, interview by author, 2 April 2001.

16. Donald Marchand, Rebecca Chung, and Katarina Paddack, "Global Growth Through Superior Information Capabilities," Case GM 953 (Lausanne, Switzerland: IMD, 2003).

17. Day, *The Market-Driven Organization*, 28–31.

18. Seán Meehan and Charlie Dawson, "Customer Responsiveness: Getting It Fast and Right Through Impatience and Intolerance," *Business Strategy Review* 13, no. 4 (2002).

19. Ibid., 26.

20. Kathleen M. Eisenhardt, Jean L. Kahwajy, and L. J. Bourgeois III, "Taming Interpersonal Conflict in Strategic Choice: How Top Management Teams Argue, But Still Get Along," in *Strategic Decisions,* ed. Vassilis Papadakis and Patrick Barwise (Norwell, MA: Kluwer, 1997), 65–83.

21. This produces a similar benefit to British Petroleum's system in which peers from different business units meet in nonhierarchical groups to discuss, debate, and take advice on their strategies. Further, they allocate fixed and scarce resources among themselves. They operate their own internal capital market, and through additional peer-group-wide stretch goals, all share a vested interest in the return on individual investments. See "Restructuring Internally for Strategic Customer Focus," *The Corporate Executive Board,* January 2003.

22. This is a verbatim quote from an episode of the award winning BBC television documentary series featuring the experiences of CEOs when they left the executive suite for a week and dealt with customers incognito. The episode in question, "Back on Site," followed Tony Pidgley, CEO of construction company Berkeley Homes, when he spent a week at one of his company's developments. "Back on Site" was screened on BBC 1 in the fall of 1997.

23. Matt Murray, "GE Chairman Goes Back to Basics—Immelt Charts New Course Focused on Core Businesses; Sales and Products Are Key," *Wall Street Journal Europe,* 6 February 2003, A1.

Chapter 7

1. Andrew S. Grove, *Only The Paranoid Survive: How to Exploit the Crisis Points That Challenge Every Company and Career* (New York: Currency Doubleday, 1996).

2. James Collins and Jerry Porras, *Built to Last* (New York: Random House, 1997).

3. Jim Dormer, *Procter & Gamble Reorganization Driving Growth* (New York: Morgan Stanley Dean Witter, 16 July 1999).

4. Internal Procter & Gamble communications.

5. Katrina Brooker and Julie Schlosser, "The Un-CEO," *Fortune,* 16 September 2002.

6. Shantanu Dutta et al., "Pricing As a Strategic Capability," *MIT Sloan Management Review* 43, no. 3 (2002).

7. Chris Warmouth, interview by author, Lausanne, Switzerland, 15 January 2003.

8. Brooker and Schlosser, "The Un-CEO."

9. Given the complexity of its core business, it is hardly surprising that Shell has sought to extend and exploit leading edge management techniques

such as scenario planning. See Pierre Wack, "Scenarios: Uncharted Waters Ahead," *Harvard Business Review* (September–October 1985): 73–89 and "Scenarios: Shooting The Rapids," *Harvard Business Review* (November–December 1985): 139–150; and, Arie P. de Geus, "Planning As Learning," *Harvard Business Review* (March–April 1988): 70–74.

10. Pat O'Driscoll, interview by author, Lausanne, Switzerland, 3 January 2003.

11. Allanna Sullivan, "Mobil Bets Drivers Pick Cappuccino over Low Prices," *Wall Street Journal,* 30 January 1995.

12. Dominique Turpin, "Kirin Brewery Co. Ltd. (A)," Case M 366 (Lausanne, Switzerland: IMD, 2002).

13. Information and quotations about Gillette's experience with innovation from Gerard J. Tellis and Peter N. Golder, "First to Market, First to Fail? Real Causes of Enduring Market Leadership," *MIT Sloan Management Review* 37, no. 2 (1996): 65.

14. Internal Duckworth Finn Grubb Waters communications concerning attitudes of car buyers, July 1994.

15. Internal Duckworth Finn Grubb Waters communications concerning attitudes of car buyers who did not own a Daewoo, March 1996.

16. Deborah Orr, "Bureaucracy Buster," *Forbes Global Business and Finance,* 25 January 1999, 40.

17. Laura Mazur, "Don't Talk Down Your Biggest Source of Sales," *Marketing Magazine,* 5 June 2003, 16.

18. Orr, "Bureaucracy Buster."

19. Peter Mouncey, review of *Building Great Customer Experiences* by Colin Shaw and John Ivens (Basingstoke, Hampshire: Palgrave Macmillan, 2002), in *Interactive Marketing* 5, no. 1 (July–September 2003): 93–98.

20. Fiona Harvey, "Warrior Wields New Weapon from Armoury," *Financial Times,* 6 August 2003.

Index

About the Authors

PATRICK BARWISE is professor of management and marketing at London Business School (LBS). He joined LBS in 1976 having spent his early career with IBM. His many publications include the books *Television and Its Audience, Accounting for Brands, Strategic Decisions, Predictions: Media,* and *Advertising in a Recession,* as well as numerous academic papers, reports, and practitioner articles on strategic investment decisions, brands, consumer and audience behavior, marketing expenditure trends, and new media. He has held a range of management roles at LBS, including faculty dean, director of alumni affairs, director of the London Executive Programme, and chairman of the Future Media Research Programme. His outside activities comprise consulting, applied research, executive development, and pro bono work, including three years as deputy chairman of the U.K. Consumers' Association. He is currently an adviser on audience research for Ofcom, the new U.K. communications regulator. He is also a frequent conference speaker and an experienced expert witness who has been involved in commercial and competition cases in London, Washington, Brussels, Paris, and Milan. Barwise holds a Masters in engineering science with economics from Oxford University, an M.B.A. from LBS, and a Ph.D. in consumer behavior from LBS.

SEÁN MEEHAN is the Martin Hilti Professor of Marketing and Change Management and director of the M.B.A. program at IMD, in Lausanne, Switzerland. His interest in the practical application of customer-centric management crystalized during his early career at Arthur Andersen, where he served clients in oil and gas, media, retail, and financial services, and at Deloitte & Touche, where he was a director of marketing. His doctoral work on customer-centric management at London Business School was recognized in the Marketing Science Institute's Alden G. Clayton Award, the Academy of Marketing's Houghton Mifflin Award, and scholarships from the Economic and Social Research Council and from LBS. Since joining IMD, he has focused on corporate strategy, customer focus, and marketing. He has designed and/or delivered management development programs for companies such as Credit Suisse, PricewaterhouseCoopers, Caterpillar Overseas S. A., Hilti, MasterCard International, Swiss Re, and Toyota. His research continues to focus on the nature and effectiveness of market orientation and customer value creation processes. Meehan holds a B.S. in business studies from Trinity College in Dublin, an M.S. in marketing from the University of Manchester Institute of Science and Technology, and a Ph.D. in marketing from LBS. He is also a certified public accountant.